Rekindled

By Pat Williams with Jerry Jenkins

The Gingerbread Man
The Power Within You

Also by Pat Williams

We Owed You One (with Bill Lyon)
Nothing But Winners (with Ken Hussar)

Rekindled

Pat and Jill Williams
with Jerry Jenkins

Fleming H. Revell Company
Old Tappan, New Jersey

Library of Congress Cataloging in Publication Data

Williams, Pat, 1940–
  Rekindled.

  1. Williams, Pat, 1940–   . 2. Williams, Jill (M.P.)
3. Christian biography—United States. 4. Marriage—
Religious aspects—Christianity. I. Williams, Jill (M.P.)
II. Jenkins, Jerry B. III. Title.
BR1700.2.W515   1985   248.8′4   85-2151
ISBN 0-8007-1417-2

To our children,
with the prayer
that they
not have to repeat our mistakes

Contents

Foreword

As a family physician I have seen so much grief, I have learned not to show my emotions. I seldom shed a tear for any reason. But the night I read *Rekindled,* I cried!

The manuscript had arrived late in the afternoon, and at eight o'clock—still at the office as usual—I decided to look it over so that I would know what to expect when I found time to read it. Prepared for scanning, my eyes slid across the first page. But, fascinated, I began to read every word, rushing from sentence to sentence, then chapter to chapter. And in the end I wept—tears of grief for the mistakes we make and tears of gratitude for what God can do in spite of those mistakes . . . and *has done.*

My first encounter with Pat Williams came in a rather mysterious phone call. Mysterious because he did not give his name, and mysterious because he somehow was able to convince my office staff to call me to the telephone anyway. The determination with which Pat was fighting to save his marriage came through even in the intensity of his voice, and I was impressed with his efforts. Little did I imagine that we would be meeting Pat and Jill in October 1984 at Jack Wyrtzen's Word of Life Camp at Schroon Lake, New York, and that the whole story would be revealed in such a way that thousands of married couples could see for themselves how love *can* be rekindled when the scriptural Love-Life principles are applied.

I am so grateful that Pat and Jill were willing to strip their souls bare in telling their story, for only in exposing themselves could others really understand the tragic plight of this handsome, gifted couple who had everything—but love.

Without love, Jill was dying emotionally, and Pat was crushed to the ground. But two factors made the difference, and these will make the difference in any troubled marriage. First, because Pat and Jill were Christians, committed to obeying God's Word, *they did not entertain the thought of divorce,* even at the lowest ebb of their relationship. Second, Pat committed himself to winning his wife's love and he went about it *in the biblical way.* It was through consistent, loving, determined application of what we call the BEST (blessing, edifying, sharing, and touching), even when there was no response at all, over a period of many months, that Pat restored his marriage. In the process he found himself falling in love with his wife—a God-fueled romantic love for her that continues to grow in depth and intensity.

What impressed us most about Pat's beautiful wife, Jill, when we met them at Schroon Lake, was the way *she* looked at him! Clearly, this is now a two-way love affair that has blessed their children and transformed every corner of their life.

Although much credit is given to the counsel in our book *Love-Life for Every Married Couple,* I have no wish to receive it personally. The Love-Life principles are found in the Scriptures, provided by God to show us how to have the kind of marriage He designed for us. And I must recognize my writing associate, Gloria Okes Perkins, for communicating these principles in the Love-Life book in such a memorable way that they have been read, understood, and applied by thousands of couples around the world.

The tears that shook me the night I read Pat and Jill's story were not only for them, but for my own story—as I remembered the heartbreaking times in the now far-distant past when my lovely wife, Gaye, and I went through some of the same experiences as the Williamses. It was these experiences that sent me to the Bible in desperation to find out what I could do as a husband to heal our situation. The Lord taught me how to love my wife, and she responded! As a result, I plunged my life into counseling others with the same truths I had learned.

The story goes on . . . Read *Rekindled,* learn from it if necessary, and then share the good news of a love-filled marriage with your friends.

ED WHEAT, M.D.
SPRINGDALE, ARKANSAS

Introduction

It would be an understandable error to assume that identifying with the love and marriage of a professional sports executive and a beauty queen might be impossible. It would be an error, nonetheless.

The husband negotiates multimillion-dollar deals with basketball stars as general manager of the Philadelphia 76ers. The wife was runner-up to Miss Illinois in 1972 and seems to have lost none of her dark, striking beauty thirteen years and four children later.

Yes, they are widely traveled. He's a much-sought-after humorist and inspirational speaker. She's a consummate violinist, vocalist, and speaker. They live in a large, quaint, nearly two-centuries-old house, and want for nothing.

But they are simply people, people with problems like everyone else. And this was proven no more graphically than by the trouble behind their closed doors. There was insensitivity, lack of communication, immaturity, frustration, depression, and finally despair—the gritty, identifiable problems and realities of many marriages.

Eventually, love was snuffed out.

Their story—the way it developed over the course of a decade—is illustrative. Read it as a way of focusing a light on your own marriage, whether it is decades old, years, months, or yet to be.

Pat and Jill Williams have made themselves uniquely vulnerable in allowing their story to be told. Indeed, they have held nothing back, sacrificing their privacy and pride for the sake of readers who might benefit from this recounting of the weaknesses in their marriage.

I met Pat in Chicago in 1972 when I interviewed him for a magazine article, Jill merely a photograph on his desk until I met her at their wedding. Eventually I wrote Pat's autobiography, *The Gingerbread Man,* and later a motivational book with him, *The Power Within You.* During those projects I noticed disconcerting clouds on the horizon of their marriage. There was evidence that Jill felt left out, that she had to badger and cajole to get a little attention. And that Pat merely smoothed her ruffled feathers as necessary.

Thus it wasn't a total surprise when Pat informed me that a crisis had bludgeoned the marriage. But how it happened and what resulted from it make a fascinating story that we pray might somehow be used to help stem the tide of failure ravaging America's marriages.

This is real-life drama, from the storybook courtship to the obliteration of emotion. But in the end, there is a miraculous stoking of coals gray and assumed cold.

Love was rejuvenated, reborn, revolutionized by the power of God through biblical principles that can be applied to any marriage. After reading the Williamses' inspiring story, you might want to turn to the questions at the end of the book to help you examine your own marriage or to use them for group study. Whether it's healthy, troubled, near death, or seemingly over, your own marriage can be enhanced and improved and—if necessary—rekindled.

JERRY JENKINS
ZION, ILLINOIS

Chapter One

The Darkest Hour— a Confrontation

"I just don't care anymore," she said, so quietly he almost couldn't hear her. Almost. "I hate this marriage. It's boring me to death." He heard that as if she'd screamed it in his ear, yet she spoke just above a whisper, staring at the floor. Pat leaned close to look in her face, realizing that she meant it, that her eyes and even her color signaled something in her he had never encountered. This wasn't something he could apologize away, something he could patch up . . . .

For Pat and Jill Williams, Sunday, December 19, 1982, has come to be known as D day in their marriage. It was the day of the bomb, the surprise attack, the confrontation that would make or break the future of their ten-year marriage.

Ironically, this D day was not planned. Pat, forty-two, was oblivious to the despair that had driven his thirty-three-year-old wife to the brink. She had long since resigned from the fight. No more whining, begging, shouting, nagging. She was finished, exiled to a bad marriage with a man who thought she was happy. Or should be.

Pat hadn't even really noticed that her tactics had changed. Perhaps the few months leading to the explosion were more peaceful than before. But that was only a relief. Maybe his young wife had merely matured, grown up, quit being so demanding, so petty, so selfish.

All he knew was that things were quieter around the house than they had been in a long time. He no longer had to defend himself from accusations, from charges that he didn't care, didn't listen, didn't praise her in public, didn't make her a priority. Maybe she seemed a little sullen lately—and there was some irrational behavior that troubled him, but basically, things were calm, and that was good.

It was a typical Sunday morning after a Philadelphia 76ers basketball game the night before. Though for some reason Jill had stopped watching the games, Pat as 76ers vice-president and general manager, of course, always did. He got to bed late at their suburban New Jersey home after watching the Sixers play the Bullets on TV from Washington. He and Jill would skip Sunday school in the morning and take their children, Jimmy, eight, Bobby, five, and Karyn, three, to church at eleven.

Pat had gone to bed unhappy. The Sixers had lost to the Washington Bullets, and three of his guards had been all but mugged by illegal moves from a Bullets agitator. Pat was angry about that and depressed by the loss.

Never down for long, by morning Pat was up and active, doing his daily Bible study and memorizing his one-a-day verse to fulfill a life commitment. He read, studied, memorized, showered and shaved, dressed, and was ready to go.

Jill, however, having as usual to get herself and three children ready, was running behind. She had fixed breakfast and cleared the table and put dinner in the oven, but despite the extra time afforded the family by skipping Sunday school, by a few minutes before eleven it was obvious they were going to be late. Again.

Jill had supervised the dressing and feeding of the boys and little Karyn. Now, as she stood before the mirror hurriedly applying her makeup, first one, then another came with a shoe-lace that had come untied or a shock of hair that wouldn't be combed into submission. "Ask your father, please! Pat! Would you help, please!"

Not volunteering, never offering, but always willing to help, "if you'd just ask me," he tied their shoes and dragged a comb through their hair as Jill hurried to dig coats out of the closet. She hated being late, but it had been ages since they were on time.

Pat remembers that he often helped with the kids before and after church. Jill's impression is that he only helped when she forced the issue. In his mind, "I wasn't just sitting there doing nothing." In her memory, he either sat in the car or stood waiting by the door.

At the office, Pat was always on time, everything was on schedule, things were precise. At home, he felt it was his responsibility to keep things moving, to keep people on track. Not so much by sharing the work load, but by motivating. Quick with a nickname, always ready with a fast quip, Pat was never at a loss for words. Often encouraging, frequently not.

His shoe-tying and hair-combing tasks accomplished, he pored over the paper, exposing box-score details to his photographic memory. Twice, as Jill scurried past, he took gentle— he thought—shots at her. "Hope you sing the hymns this morning." Sometimes she did, sometimes she didn't. Lately she hadn't.

She ignored him. He hadn't thought much about why he said it. Looking back, he thinks he was only trying to keep her moving, get her motivated, get her out the door so they could all get to church.

Jill hurried past again. She had quickly regained her figure after having Karyn, and she looked as good as she had in years. Indeed, she could have worn the same clothes she wore in 1972 when she won the talent (violin) and bathing-suit competitions on her way to being first runner-up to Miss Illinois.

She had always dressed well, and her dark hair and eyes and clear complexion set off perfect, gleaming teeth. A mention of her beauty from Pat would have stopped her in her tracks, made her day, maybe put a smile on her face. Instead, despite the natural beauty, there was a set to the jaw, a weariness in the eyes, a stiffness in the gait. "Haven't seen you studying your Bible lately," he called after her.

She turned to glare at him but had neither the time nor the energy to say what she thought. He glanced up briefly, just long enough to realize he had cut her deeply with that remark. "It was as if her lights went out," he recalls. He got the icy, silent treatment for the rest of the morning.

They arrived ten minutes late to their little house of worship. Often Jill had concerned Pat by not singing out during congregational hymns, but this time she didn't sing at all. Didn't open her mouth.

Jill had perfected the silent treatment over the years to where she could make it perfectly clear to Pat that he was in the doghouse, while charming the socks off her friends and co-parishioners. And even though this would be a day unlike any other day in their marriage, she didn't know that yet. And the routine was the same. Pat got the ice; everyone else got the warm fuzzies.

On the way out it was a smile and a "Hi, hello, how are you?" for everyone, and Pat and Jill gradually lost contact with each other. Pat wanted to get home. He was hungry, there were games to watch on television, and he figured he'd probably have to have a little fence-mending session with Jill.

There had been a few of those over the years. When he couldn't deflect the badgering or the sullenness or the crying or the silence, he would sit her down to find out what was wrong, apologize for whatever unintentional thing he had said or done, and try to get on with life. If she wasn't better on the way home, if things didn't loosen up a little in the car, it was apparent he was going to have to try to smooth things over. It might even require taking her to dinner some night soon. Anything to keep the peace and get things back to normal. Normal was fine with Pat. Normal was killing Jill.

He sat in the car in the parking lot, nodding and waving to friends, not wanting to be responsible for getting home any later than necessary. Jill was rounding up all three kids, a chore she knew by now was expected of her. But if there had been any possibility of a thaw in her mood, it was obliterated when she found Pat waiting impatiently in the car while she herded the kids into the backseat.

On the way home, Pat attempted a few forays into the wall she had erected. She didn't look at him. She answered with as few words as possible. She pretended to be preoccupied with the children.

Their normal course on Sunday was to eat out so they could get home and get Karyn down for her afternoon nap. As it happened, however, Jill had prepared a lunch that day. It was during that lunch when Pat realized that, indeed, this was a spat that needed patching up. She was so cold and quiet during the meal, he recalls, "it was as if she wasn't a factor at all."

She put Karyn down for her nap and returned to the kitchen to clean up. Pat clapped Jimmy on the shoulder. "Why don't you and Bobby go play in the family room while I talk to Mother."

Jill felt a flutter in the pit of her stomach as Jimmy and Bobby disappeared and Pat led her to the living room. He had said he wanted to talk to her with such an ominous finality that she wondered if she would be able to fake her way out of a confrontation as she so often did. Hiding her fear and discomfort, she immediately threw on a frustrated, impatient face. She wanted him to know she was wishing he'd get on with it so she could finish in the kitchen and get a nap before her concert that night at church.

Pat was convinced that his two verbal shots that morning had hurt her, and he merely wanted to apologize to reestablish peace in the home. It was bad enough that he had to go to the 76ers Christmas party that night and would miss her concert; that made it difficult for both of them, having to make excuses for each other. He didn't need another rift between them.

Jill pulled her hand away from his and headed for the couch directly across from the green and white love seat where he was about to sit. She didn't want to be next to him, but he quickly rose and guided her, a hand on each shoulder, to sit with him. She pressed her lips tight and wouldn't look at him.

"Now, Jill, what's wrong?"

She shook her head and spoke softly. "Nothing."

A meaningless, typical response, to which Pat could have responded a hundred different ways. He could have stood and embraced her and said, "Jill, that's wonderful. I was afraid you were upset because of what I said this morning. Forgive me and let's go on." He could have said, "Fine, if you aren't going to tell me, then there's nothing I can do about it."

But he felt he had caused the problem; it was a little spat, and he wanted to take care of it, to handle it properly. "No," he said. "This time I'm not going to accept 'nothing.' Something's been bothering you for hours and I want you to tell me what it is."

Inwardly, Jill flinched. "Nothing," she repeated, desperate to keep from having to tell the whole truth. Because this time it wasn't something he'd said or done, an argument, an oversight, an offense. It was everything, and it had been building for the last two months on a foundation that had been poured the day they were married. She stood to leave, but he stopped her.

"Jill, I want you to tell me. We're going to sit here and get this straight if it takes all night."

"What do you mean? Why?"

"Listen, you're not singing in church, you're not having your devotions, you're snapping at the kids. Tell me what's wrong."

Pat still thought that if he could get the reason out of her, it would concern his unkind remarks that morning. He and Jill still cringe at the thought that he could have let her off the hook by suggesting that or by letting her head back to the kitchen insisting nothing was wrong.

Jill hadn't planned to say what she said next. It surprised her as much as it did Pat, but it didn't shock her, didn't cut her to the bone the way it did him. Her shocking and cutting had come gradually over the years. He was getting his all at once.

"I just don't care anymore," she said, so quietly he almost couldn't hear her. Almost. "I hate this marriage. It's boring me to death." He heard that as if she'd screamed it in his ear, yet she spoke just above a whisper, staring at the floor. Pat leaned close to look in her face, realizing that she meant it, that her eyes and even her color signaled something in her he had never encountered. This wasn't something he could apologize away, something he could patch up with a baby-sitter and a dinner in Philly.

"I give up," she managed.

"Jill, I'm sorry. I didn't mean to upset you with what I said this morning. I apologize for that." But he could tell, as she waved that off with a flick of her hand, that it went much deeper.

"I don't even know if I love you anymore. I don't even know if I ever loved you."

Pat felt as if his heart had stopped. "Really, Jill?" he said, his throat tight. "What can I do? What can we do?"

Jill began a soft litany of the countless complaints she had registered for so many years, never having felt she had really gotten his attention long enough to get any response. He looked at her sadly and she wondered if he was finally hearing her for the first time.

If he had only been listening all those years, the charges echoing in his mind wouldn't have come as revelations now:

You don't really care about this marriage.

Why should I try to be a good wife? You never notice anything anyway.

We never do anything together unless it's something you want to do.

You never share anything with me, your work, your Bible study, your dreams, your goals.

Why can't you remember the little things, the special days unless I circle them in red on the calendar?

You talk to me like I'm a Philadelphia sportswriter.

Couldn't you ever come home a little early just to be with me? Or come and pick me up and take me to the game instead of leaving me to find my own way there with friends?

You never hold my hand anymore. You never touch me unless you want something more.

You never say nice things to me in front of people.

You're okay with the kids only after I've asked you five or six times.

You never act as if my words are important. You never really listen. You either interrupt or don't let me talk at all when we're with other people.

I don't want things. I want you. Don't give me crumbs. I want the real thing. You've never made a one hundred percent commitment to me. You've never really given me you.

Pat was listening now. For years she had suggested marriage seminars and marriage books, but he had really not seen the need. To him, his marriage was fine. Sure, his wife was a little moody at times, hard to please, maybe a little spoiled. But they always worked it out. She was a rock, always there when he needed her, running a good house, raising the kids, often singing at his speaking engagements. Until that moment, when Jill finally surprised herself by letting it all tumble out, Pat Williams thought he had a great marriage. Even an ideal one.

"Jill, how can you say you don't love me? I love *you.*"

"I didn't really know you when we got married," she said, if anything even more quietly now. "I didn't really know you as a person. It was fairly quick. Maybe I made a mistake. How do I know that I didn't?"

"I know *I* didn't," Pat said, desperate to keep her talking. "I know you're the girl God picked out for me."

It was as if she hadn't heard him. "I'm not going to leave because the kids would be devastated. I'll stick around. I know as a Christian that divorce isn't an option. Maybe I should go away for a while."

"Do you think that would help? If you think that would help, it would be fine. Do what you have to do to get your act together, Jill, because we're going to work this thing out. Should we talk to someone?"

"Who would we talk to, Pat? Anyone around here thinks we're Mr. and Mrs. Joe Christian with our whole thing together."

"Should we talk to someone we don't know, who doesn't know us?"

"I don't even want to think about it."

"We have to think about it. We have to do something."

"Don't worry, I won't leave you. I'll cook your meals and wash your clothes and take care of the kids. But I can't enjoy being with you anymore. I've given up."

"What do you mean, you've given up?"

"I can't seem to get you to spend time with me or respond to me, but I know biblically I have to stay with you, so I'll stay. I can't promise any emotion. Don't expect any response or any real feeling from me, because I don't have anything left."

Pat was eager to talk about arranging for a vacation for her, anything to help, anything to keep her talking, anything to get her to look at him, to speak up, to stay there. But she had talked enough, and all she could think of was getting upstairs for a nap. "Think about where you might like to go to get away for a while," he said. "Or who we might talk to."

She nodded without enthusiasm and heaved a heavy sigh. "I'm very tired. I need a nap before I sing tonight." And she trudged upstairs alone, leaving Pat in shock. He realized as he sat there that he had just seen his wife die emotionally. It was absolutely the most frightening thing he'd ever seen in his life.

She wanted out, she didn't care, she wasn't sure she loved him. That hurt. Part of him still wished he hadn't said what he'd said that morning, but down deep he knew it went much further than that. He felt totally rejected and could only hope she'd made her statements in anger and that she didn't really mean them. He hoped that after her nap, she'd feel better.

For Jill's part, all she knew was that she had finally gotten his attention, but she sincerely didn't care anymore. She was relieved to have finally quit living the lie, at least in front of Pat. That night, she would live it before her own congregation, smiling and singing Christmas songs. She hated being a phony, so she chose only general songs that didn't hit too close to home. That she could even survive the concert in the mental and emotional state she was in was miraculous in itself.

Pat had checked in on the children and then ran hard and long that afternoon while Jill napped. The exercise in the frigid winter air was invigorating, but he was unable to run off his fear, his sense of dread, of failure, of rejection. He had been rocked to the core, and he had no idea what he was going to do.

Jill was no better after her nap. She couldn't look at him, wouldn't talk to him, wouldn't respond to his good-bye peck as he headed for the Christmas party. Usually the life of such parties, as one of the bosses and a nationally known humorist, Pat was only able to sleepwalk through the niceties. He was distracted, nervous, hollow.

He felt the need to hurry home on this snowy night. Maybe after her concert Jill would be in a better mood to talk. She might accept his sincere apology, and maybe take back some of the things she had said.

It wasn't terribly late when he arrived home. But the house was dark. The old hardwood floors squeaked and groaned. She had to know he was there. But when he entered the bedroom, there was no response. Could she be sound asleep? It appeared so. He undressed on the verge of tears.

One thing the Philadelphia 76ers vice-president and general manager had never had trouble doing was falling asleep. Anyone who ever knew him in any capacity said he was one of the busiest, most fast-paced, hard-driving executives they'd ever seen, totally committed, even obsessed with every area of life. He worked hard and long and he slept good and sound.

But not this night. He slid between the sheets that had never seemed icier and let his eyes grow accustomed to the dark. Jill slept with her back to him. He gently rested his hand on her side, just above her hip, and held his breath to see if he could detect any change in her breathing. She didn't stir. He rolled to his back, his hands behind his head, and stared wide-eyed at the ceiling in the darkness.

He needed his sleep. The holidays were a busy time in the 76ers office. But his well-ordered and disciplined life was unraveling all at once. To Jill it may have been happening for years. For Pat, the trauma was only hours old.

He and Jill were coming up on their unmerriest Christmas ever. What had he done? Where had he failed? How could this have happened?

Chapter Two

Looking for Mr. Right

Jill Marie was the firstborn child of Emil and Mildred Paige. Four years later, sister Debbie was born, completing the family. Devout Christians, the insurance agent and his church-organist wife raised their daughters in Riverside, Illinois, a quaint suburb of winding, tree-lined streets fifteen miles west of Chicago. The Paiges were of Czech stock, Bohemians with a Gaelic name.

Jill describes her parents as longtime, family-type, second-generation Christians. For many years Jill enjoyed having three living grandparents, who provided a rich heritage of faith in Christ. From as far back as she can remember, Jill was God conscious. God and Jesus and the Holy Spirit and church and Christian music and prayer and a tranquil home were givens in her young life.

She was an ideal, typical firstborn, a parent pleaser, quiet, shy, obedient, studious. She loved to play church, sing songs, go to Sunday school, read her Bible, and pray. She simply loved church, became a Christian at age five at a service preached by then evangelist and chalk artist George Sweeting, and never had second thoughts about it. "At times I thought I was abnormal because everyone was going through doubt or rebellion. But I never did. I never questioned. I was the good girl."

Jill inherited her mother's looks and temperament, and

while she has always had a strong relationship with her father, she was closest to her mother. Debbie looked more like her father and was a "daddy's girl."

Jill remembers the family as close and affectionate, and while she is much more physically demonstrative with her own children, she wasn't aware of a lack of that in her childhood. Love was not verbalized as much as it was shown. And she always preferred being with her family than with anyone else, playing table games at home, just spending time with one another. Whatever the comfortable, middle-income Paiges may have lacked in luxuries, they never missed an annual family vacation.

In fact the only cloud in the sky of Jill's memory is the rivalry between her and her younger sister. Rivalry may be too strong a word, because Debbie may not even have seen it that way. All Jill knew was that people seemed to favor Debbie. Debbie was the one with the dimples and the blue eyes and the naturally curly Shirley Temple hair. To Jill, Debbie was cuter and everyone liked her better—outsiders anyway. Mr. and Mrs. Paige were careful never to appear to favor one over the other or to imply that one was cuter. In fact, it's unlikely that there was anything plain about Jill; it's just that her sister was four years younger and would naturally attract more attention when they were little.

The fact that people outside the family pay more attention to her younger children bothers Jill even today. "I'd like to remind them that there's nothing ordinary or unattractive about the older kids," she says. "But I guess it's human nature to make a bigger fuss over the little ones."

Whenever Jill was asked what she wanted to be when she grew up, she had a stock answer: "Just a plain old mother." The words were always the same, and as mundane as they may appear, she meant them and said them because of her own mother. Mildred Paige never worked outside the home, was always there, made the family her top priority, and made motherhood and homemaking seem the most attractive occupation for her daughter. Jill loved that her mom was just a "plain old

mother," and there was nothing she would rather be. As soon
as she was old enough to maneuver around the house and pretend, she imagined herself the owner of a huge orphanage with
dozens of children. She was everyone's mama and took care of
them all.

Jill loved music almost from the beginning. She sang her
first solo in church when she was four, started piano lessons the
next year, took up the violin at age ten, and had private lessons
for eight years. While in junior high she auditioned and was
selected for the Youth Orchestra of Greater Chicago that
played in Orchestra Hall. She spent nearly every Saturday
until she graduated from high school practicing the whole day.

She was a good student, skipping second grade and coasting
through high school without aggressively applying herself to
her studies. She did well but was not an honor-roll student. She
sang in the choir and went to school ball games with a few girlfriends, but basically she was a loner.

"The fact is, I hated high school."

Her class numbered about four hundred and fifty students,
and her recollection is that she knew just three or four, "and
one was my cousin." Even with the Youth Orchestra, she preferred eating her lunch alone. "I was nothing in high school."
She dated only church boys and was really interested in none
of them. Family, church, and music were all that motivated
her. She didn't run in the right circles to be noticed as the type
of beauty who might become homecoming or prom queen.

Despite the talent she had honed though years of practice,
she never had it in her mind to become a musical performer.
Her violin teacher thought she showed great promise and was
horrified when she ignored a full scholarship to Northwestern
University, deciding to attend Sterling College, in Kansas, a
small (400 students) Presbyterian school. But it was a decision
that changed Jill's life.

In the fall of 1966, the pretty, talented, smart freshman was
suddenly a big fish in a little pond. Students and faculty and
staff loved her. Her grades put her on the dean's list, and she
was involved in everything from class office, to the concert and

touring choirs, as well as in a variety of small, touring gospel groups. She was surprised to be named both Valentine Queen and Homecoming Queen. "I thought everyone always voted only for the cheerleaders."

She was no more comfortable in front of crowds—especially alone—and down deep she still wasn't convinced that she was anything special. Like many women, Jill had a problem with self-esteem. It surprised her that people thought she was good-looking enough for the honors she was receiving. If heads turned when she entered the room, she assumed something was wrong with her makeup or hair.

While the potentially image-healing compliments weren't really reaching or impacting Jill's psyche, she was enjoying the attention and the activity. Having always sincerely felt she had played second fiddle to Debbie's dimples, Jill was slowly gaining confidence on learning there were things people appreciated about her as well.

But when the dean of women told her that the local Jaycees had asked about potential contestants for the Miss Rice County Pageant (one of the feeders into the Miss Kansas, and eventually the Miss America, Pageant), Jill thought the dean merely wanted her to recommend someone.

"No, I want *you* to enter," the dean said.

"Me?"

Jill wasn't playing dumb or being falsely modest. It really hadn't occurred to her that being popular and considered attractive on a small college campus should make anyone think she was beauty-pageant material. When she asked her parents why the dean would suggest such a thing, they encouraged her to try it.

The summer after her freshman year, then, she entered her first pageant and finished first runner-up. And she caught pageant fever. People critical of the Miss America Pageant get an argument from Jill, who is sold on the positive impact the nationwide program has on the contestants, both financially and motivationally. Many of her fondest memories and longest-lasting friendships began at pageants.

The next year, Jill won the Miss Rice County title and finished among the top ten for Miss Kansas, being named the most talented instrumentalist. She relinquished her Miss Rice County crown the following year, but she emceed the pageant, performed, judged, and even chaperoned the new winner to the Miss Kansas competition.

While there was still a lot of "why me?" running through her mind, Jill had gained confidence in front of crowds and was much more at ease making friends. She never shook the initial shyness that came with finding herself in new situations and groups of people, and realization of her own physical beauty is something she acknowledges in her head but which has to this day never reached her core. "I appreciate that people think so, and I like to dress up and think I look good, but I have never really accepted—for myself—the fact that I'm anything special to look at."

Jill had begun to date more and more and went through a short-lived engagement to a young man she finally decided just wasn't right for her. She still wanted to be just a plain old mother, but without any particular prospects or guarantees, she majored in education and looked forward to a teaching career—"but not all my life."

When she graduated during the summer of 1970, she was still old-fashioned enough to believe that a single girl should live at home with her parents until she married. It was a little different and felt strange to be at home without Debbie, who had left for her first year of college. Jill busied herself by looking for work. She applied to more than a hundred Chicago-area schools for an elementary-teaching position. School districts, however, were in the middle of cutbacks and declining enrollment, while colleges were still pumping out teachers by the thousands.

The competition was fierce for the few jobs open, and up until the last week of August, Jill had gotten the courtesy of even a negative reply from only a handful of schools. Just when she decided that the Lord wanted her to stop being so anxious and to just rest in Him, she was offered a third-grade class at Tioga Elementary School in Bensenville, thirty miles from home.

It was during that year that Jill started thinking seriously about her real life's ambition. In her heart of hearts, she still wanted to be just a plain old mother. She was dating frequently and even enjoyed a few fairly serious relationships. In fact, she received several marriage proposals. But when she thought of the complication of her first broken engagement, she was slow to respond, and indeed, turned down every one.

It wasn't that these weren't impressive guys. Some were wealthy, others very spiritual. Most fit her unwritten list of qualities she wanted in a husband:

Never been married
Christian
Friendly
Good sense of humor
Good job
Ability to be spiritual leader in the home

Throw in tall, dark, and handsome, and Jill wondered if it wasn't too much to hope for. But there *were* those who seemed to qualify. Somehow, as eager as they were for her to say yes, she was waiting for God's timing, God's man. There was something missing, something more she wanted, something she couldn't quite articulate, that she didn't see in any of the many who would have jumped at the chance to marry her.

It wasn't long before Jill became preoccupied with finding Mr. Right, and the stream of wedding invitations she received from friends and acquaintances didn't help. Good grief, here it was the middle of 1971 and she was already twenty-two, and still single! Her search became a frequent topic of conversation at home, and her father always reminded her, "He's out there somewhere. You'll find him."

She knew the truth of Jeremiah 33:3 that if she called on the Lord, He would show her "great and mighty things." She only wanted one. She also agreed with the truth of Genesis 2:18 that it is not good for man (or woman) to be alone.

She tried not to be impatient, especially with the pithy little quote on her mother's refrigerator staring her in the face every day: "God always gives His best to those who leave the choice with Him." Jill felt she *was* leaving the choice with God by not reacting impulsively to the proposals she had received. But once she had made her decision on the current crop of hopefuls, there didn't seem to be any more around.

She enjoyed going places with her parents, but she would rather have had a date. And better, she would rather have been getting to know *the* right guy. She was convinced that all the good-looking Christian guys were married already—either that or she had already decided they weren't right for her, and as much as she tried to avoid it, she was growing cynical. The lovely, young Jill Paige, Miss Everything, everyone's favorite teacher, the parent pleaser from way back, was actually becoming a bit difficult to live with. She even started visiting other churches to see if there were any prospects. She would never go alone, of course. She couldn't remember ever having ventured out by herself. With all her experience and honors, she was still scared to enter a new situation without someone with her. The harder she looked and the less she found, the more depressed, lonely, and irritable she became.

In the fall, after her second year of teaching at Tioga had begun, she and her parents decided to fill a free October evening by attending a Sixteen Singing Men concert at the First Baptist Church in Wheaton. Somehow they arrived way too early. The church was open, but no one else was there yet.

With little to do but mosey around, Jill found herself idly reading the bulletin boards. "Mom," she said, "look at this article. Pat Williams is going to speak at a banquet here."

"Who's Pat Williams?"

"Says here he's general manager of the Chicago Bulls basketball team." She had forgotten that he was the man who gave his testimony at the Billy Graham crusade in Chicago in June when she was in the choir. Jill had seen him from behind and was with a date anyway, so she hadn't given him a second thought until now. She didn't even remember what he had

said. Neither had she realized then that he was both a bachelor
and a Christian. But that's what the article said.

"Maybe I could go to this banquet," she said, as her father
peeked over their shoulders at the bulletin board.

"Nope," he said. "It's old news. See? The banquet was last
month."

Later she told her mother, pretending to be kidding, but inwardly dead serious, "That's the kind of guy I'm going to
marry. Pat Williams." Her mother laughed. Jill knew it was
silly to think that a small-town girl could marry a big-time
professional sports executive. But there was nothing wrong
with dreaming.

On her way back and forth to work every day, Jill enjoyed
listening to WMBI, the radio station of Moody Bible Institute.
One morning she heard an announcement that the great bass
singer Frank Boggs was to have a Thanksgiving evening concert at Moody Church, where Warren Wiersbe had just been
installed as the new pastor. She wondered if her parents might
want to go with her to hear him. Until, that is, she heard the
second part of the announcement. Pat Williams would also be
speaking.

"My ears perked up," she recalls. "I had heard of him. I had
seen him from behind. I knew a little about him from the clip-
ping I had read. And I remembered not only that he was a
bachelor and a Christian, but also what I had told my mother."

The wheels began to turn, and Jill decided she was going to
take a bold step. She was going to get down to Moody Church,
alone, and figure out a way to introduce herself to this Pat
Williams.

It would be no small feat. While she was determined to go
through with it, it was one thing to play a violin before a big
crowd and judges and quite another to approach a bachelor
alone. Remember, this was a woman who believed a single girl
should live with her parents.

Thanksgiving was always a big event in the Paige family.
That year they convened at Jill's aunt's house in Wheaton,
where twelve enjoyed the big meal. After dinner, Jill pulled her

mother aside and said casually, as if she'd just thought of it, "I think I'll run down to Moody Church to hear Frank Boggs this evening."

Her mother, who knew Jill like a book, couldn't suppress a twinkle. "Do you want me to go with you?"

"No, that's all right. You stay here."

It was a first, and all the way to Chicago in the darkness, Jill reminded herself that even though she was not yet twenty-three, it seemed as though her friends were passing her by. Some had been married long enough already to begin sending out birth announcements.

The closer she got to Chicago, the more nervous she became. *How am I going to do this?* she wondered. *How does one maneuver to be in the right place at the right time to meet someone like Pat Williams?* She knew she should have a plan, but she didn't know where to begin.

It was cold and dark as she parked and hurried into the huge auditorium. Thousands of people were there, and Jill knew that to have any chance of meeting Pat, she would have to be up near the front. She sat in the third row. *A little obvious, maybe,* she told herself.

Up to that point, she had never seen Pat Williams, even in a photograph. When she finally caught sight of him, she was overwhelmed. He was a sharp dresser, not overly flashy, but tasteful, expensive, classy. His dark hair was styled just so. He was trim and athletic, confident almost to the point of being cocky, but not quite.

Pat was very popular in Chicago and seemed to have his whole life together, spiritually and otherwise. He was an excellent and funny speaker, keeping everyone's attention. She was fascinated by his ability to stand calmly before such a crowd and be at ease. But nothing of what he said impacted her. She couldn't calm herself enough to concentrate. He was all and more than she had hoped, and she just knew she had to meet him. But how? And where? What if he just disappeared after the concert?

Almost before she knew it, and before she had time to de-

vise a plan of attack, the concert was over and people were fil-
ing out. She nearly panicked. "I can't do it," she said out loud.
"But I have to do it. That's why I came. But what am I going to
say?" She was barely aware that people were staring at her as
they left, obviously wondering whom she was talking to.

"I had never talked to myself before in my life," she says.
"And I don't think I have since either. But I was desperate.
Here I had come all this way, and the thing was over. And I
didn't have a plan."

But there was Pat, sitting in the front row, about three seats
in from the aisle, signing autographs for some boys, dozens of
them. "That's it," Jill said, "I'll get in line. But I've got to come
up with something better than, 'Hi, I'm single and here's my
phone number.'"

Chapter Three

Dating

As Jill moved toward the front of the auditorium, she remembered hearing an announcement that Pat was willing to speak to various groups in his efforts to promote the Bulls in Chicago, and that he would be happy to share his testimony too. As she went to the back of the line of little boys, an idea came to her.

Although there were still several boys in front of her and she had plenty of time to prepare her words, it seemed the kids were moving too rapidly. Her heart cracked against her ribs, and suddenly there was just one youngster between her and THE Pat Williams. Was she ready? She wasn't sure. Maybe the boy would ask some questions, keep Pat talking. Maybe another would come up looking for an autograph and she would let him cut in front of her. But no, the boy was as nervous as she and just stood silently as Pat signed his autograph. Then he hurried away to his parents and Pat looked up to see who was next.

But what's this? Not the curly head of an elementary-school boy but a young woman. Pat's eyes traveled upward and he quickly stood. She extended her hand and took a deep breath, gushing forth without a pause, "Hi, I'm Jill Paige and I teach third grade at Tioga Elementary School in Bensenville and the boys in my class would never forgive me if I didn't get your autograph."

Pat remembers thinking it was a little odd that this good-

looking gal would introduce herself, but he shook her hand,
said, "Sure," and signed her program.

"Do you speak to school children?"

Pat looked up at her as he handed the program back. "Yes, I
do that."

"Would you be willing to come and speak to my students
one day?"

"Sure, I'd be very happy to."

"How would I get in touch with you?"

"You could call the office. Or I could call you. Why don't
you give me your number and I'll get back to you."

Jill still wonders how she stayed on her feet. He seemed as
shy as she was. She might have wished he'd been a little more
"take charge," but there was something intriguing about this
less-than-confident one-on-one aspect of him too. All the
while, Pat never assumed anything other than that he had received a straightforward request for an autograph and to speak
to some students. In fact, he thought he had been pretty
smooth in weaseling a phone number out of this good-looking
woman.

Jill really wanted to hang around to see if he might be looking for a late-dinner companion, but she wasn't about to ask
him if he was hungry. She realized she was dreaming to think
he'd suggest such a thing to a total stranger, so when she
couldn't think of anything else to say, she left him with a "Nice
to meet you," and floated to her car.

As soon as the door was shut, she squealed with delight, not
so much because she thought she had bowled him over or even
impressed him at all—she wasn't sure she had—but simply because she had accomplished her mission. She had done it, she
had succeeded, she had mustered enough courage to introduce
herself, and that made her feel good. She found herself hum-
ming Frank Boggs's standard, "I Have Come From the Darkness to the Light," and she prayed that that might be true of
her too. She had already come to the "light of redemption from
sin." But she wanted to come out of the darkness of singleness
into the light as Pat Williams's wife.

Now, would he call? And if he did, would it be to see about speaking to the kids? It was a dark, wet, cold Thanksgiving night, but she wasn't conscious of the tires on the pavement. It would be after eleven when she got home to Riverside, and she knew her mother would be up waiting for her.

Jill was grinning as she came through the door. "Mother, I'm going to marry Pat Williams." Mrs. Paige smiled, but kept from laughing. She listened to the whole story, and no doubt found Jill's conclusion a bit premature, but she promised to be nice if the young man happened to call when Jill wasn't home. At first Jill hadn't thought too much about whether he would call. But having the Friday after Thanksgiving off and the weekend to think and pray about it—with the whole family—she became obsessed with the idea.

Everyone was coached on what to say and how to sound in the event that they answered instead of Jill, which was only possible if she wasn't home. As it was, she felt as if she were sitting by the phone. Yet, just as in a B movie, each time it rang she put her hand on the receiver and let it ring fully twice. Just before the start of the third ring, she'd casually answer it. No sense in sounding too eager, How many friends and acquaintances noticed the disappointment in her voice when she discovered they weren't "him"?

On Sunday between church services she spent every spare minute within earshot of the phone. No luck. With each day that passed, she became more pessimistic about his call. *Am I really going to have to call him and ask him to speak to my kids?* she wondered. She decided she just wouldn't do that.

The next week she was to teach all day and attend the Bill Gothard Institute in Basic Youth Conflicts Seminar every night. She raced home from work Monday afternoon to get ready for the seminar, but mostly to find out if you-know-who had called. "No," her mother said. "Sorry." Jill couldn't remember ever having been as disappointed, and helpless. She simply wouldn't call him, but if he didn't call soon, she was going to burst.

She found the Gothard seminar fascinating and was glad she

had committed the time, but again, when she arrived home and there was no phone message, she was crushed. The next day at work, she began the process of telling herself she should give it up. It was too much to hope for anyway. She'd most likely made a fool of herself. He had probably seen her coming a mile away and knew what she was up to. No doubt he hadn't given her a second thought. Why would he?

Jill and her parents had actually already prayed that if it was God's will that she be married to Pat Williams, He would work things out. She realized how preliminary, how anticipatory that was, but they also believed that if it wasn't God's will, He would make that clear too. Now she was afraid that maybe that's what was happening.

It was too early to suppress all hope that Pat might call even that day, but she knew she'd better start preparing herself for the big letdown. As she pulled into the driveway, she forgot her self-admonitions and was eager to hear if there had been any messages. But her mother wasn't home!

She couldn't believe it. Her mother was usually there. What if he had called when no one was home? He'd probably just give up and never try again. Then she noticed the three-by-five card leaning against the phone. Her mother had printed three words in big, bold letters: GUESS WHO CALLED?

Guess who called! She *knew* who called, but what was she supposed to do with *that* message? Call him back? Had he left instructions? Said he would call back? Would like her to call? And where should she call him? At the office? At home? She wouldn't even dare try until she heard from her mother what she was supposed to do.

Her mother didn't get home until after dinner when it was time for Jill to leave for the seminar. "He would like you to call him at the office," Mrs. Paige reported. Obviously, it was too late for that, and it would be very late when she got home from the meeting. She wouldn't be able to call him until her lunch break the next day!

Wednesday she got to school early, but that just made the morning drag even more. What if all he wanted was to know when he should come and speak to the class? That would be all right, she decided. At least he had called, and she would have another opportunity to see him and maybe impress him. Somehow.

By the time Jill got to the pay phone in the gym, it was all she could do to catch her breath and calm herself. Her hand shook as she dropped the coins into the slot. She figured she'd have to go through a switchboard and then Pat's secretary, not realizing that he had a policy of answering his own phone so that any fan had access to the boss any time he was in.

After asking for Pat Williams, the next voice she heard was his. "Oh, uh, hi," she said. "This is Jill Paige. I'm just returning your call from yesterday."

Pat said he was wondering if she was free for dinner Friday night. There was an ever-so-brief pause as Jill let it sink in. What she had wanted more than anything else ever in her life, more than the Miss Rice County title, more than the Miss Kansas title, more than any date or gift or anything, had just been offered by the man on whom she had set her sights. Dinner Friday night? Or course! Perfect.

"I'm sorry," she said, not believing the words coming from her own mouth. She didn't even sound disappointed. "I'd love to, but I'm involved in the Bill Gothard seminar, which goes through Saturday."

Horrified at herself for not jumping at the chance to go out with Pat, Jill knew she couldn't break a commitment. That simply wasn't the way she was made. Immediately she began listening intently to see if she had put him off, offended him, disappointed him. Would he suggest another date, another time? There was nothing else she would let stand in the way.

She detected a little admiration, maybe, that she was attending a Gothard seminar—something Pat had done once too—and that she was committed to it. But through all the small talk that followed there was no hint of another call, another invitation. "Maybe another time," he said, but unconvincingly. She didn't think he sounded terribly disappointed; she certainly was.

But he *was* disappointed when he hung up. He'd dated enough to know when he'd been rejected. Not that he felt it was personal. He believed her excuse, still, he had been turned down. He wouldn't dwell on it. He'd just put it out of his mind for now. Maybe he'd call her again some time. He was pretty busy right then. It was the middle of the season after all.

Pat had once had a blind date with a beautiful girl at Wake Forest. She went on to become a state beauty-pageant winner too, ironically enough. He didn't know how he had impressed her, but she had certainly impressed him. In fact, when he got back to his room that night, he knew he had it bad. He was in love. This was it. He wanted nothing more than to see that girl again. But when he next saw her and asked her out on a "real" date—no blind date, no double date, just you and me and for real—she turned him down flat. Sort of a "No, thanks, and best of luck to you, kid."

So there would be no more immediate decisions on Pat Williams's part. No falling for someone before he was sure it went both ways. No setting himself up for rejection or big disappointments.

Jill had found him vague and noncommittal, but he *had* said maybe some other time. She hoped and prayed and dreamed about that, discussing it with her parents at length, even as far as talking about how nice it was that he was headquartered in Chicago, so she wouldn't be too far away if they did get married.

Her parents humored her in that. There was no harm in it, they felt. It could happen. Why not? Their daughter was special, lovely, devout. God could be pleased to give her such a gift. Stranger things had happened. They just hoped she wouldn't be disappointed, that Pat hadn't led her on, that she hadn't run him off by excusing herself from his first dinner invitation.

The first week of December dragged by, and Jill talked and daydreamed about Pat every minute she was home. But no phone messages awaited her. In fact, she would wait a whole month before he called again.

By New Year's eve, Jill had given up hope. She sat with her parents in her uncle's church for a watch-night service and tried to put it all into perspective. The problem was, she wasn't ready to let it die. It hurt too much. How could she have been so close, and then see him slip through her fingers? What could she have done differently?

At the stroke of midnight her father leaned over and gave her a New Year's kiss. Always quick with a rhyme or some doggerel, he said, "Seventy-two is for you."

Jill shrugged and sneered. "Right," she said, sarcastically. She knew immediately she had hurt his feelings, but it had been almost a month since she had talked to Pat. If '72 was for her, Pat Williams apparently wasn't going to be part of it. She decided to quit wasting her energy hoping and worrying. She didn't stop praying, but his name wasn't mentioned around the house anymore. It wasn't a fun topic, and Jill was becoming miserable to live with.

Wednesday night, January 5, the Paige family was celebrating Emil Paige's birthday in their Riverside home. They were playing Scrabble. Jill, who was by now basically unhappy and cynical about her future, hated delays once a game got started. But the phone kept ringing. First it was for her father. "Yes, thank you, no I don't feel any older. Thanks for calling." Then it was for her mother. Then Dad again. Jill was rapping her nails on the table. *This is ridiculous,* she thought. Two more in a row were for her dad and when he returned, he said, "The next one's for you."

She hardly looked at him. She just said, "Right," a repeat of her sarcasm five nights before. She didn't like herself much right then, but she was beyond cheering. The phone rang. "Oh, for Pete's sake!" she complained. Her dad answered it and came back to the table, smiling.

"Like I said," he told her. "It's for you."

"Who is it?" she grumbled, rising slowly.

"Pat Williams."

She slumped back down, her face nearly drained of color. "You're kidding!"

Her father helped her stand. "I'm not kidding, now get to the phone!"

All was forgiven before she even picked up the receiver. "Jill, how are you?"

"Fine." [Now.]

"How's your school teaching going?"

"Oh, just fine." [Let's get on with it!]

"I've been terribly busy this season."

"Really? Oh, I imagine!" [I should hope so after not calling me for over a month!]

"We have home games this Friday and a week from Saturday, and I thought if you would be able to get a ride to one of them, I'd be glad to see you and we could grab a bite and I'd drive you home."

"I love basketball." [What kind of a klutz is this guy, asking me to find my own way there?]

"Which night would be convenient for you, Jill?"

"This Friday night would be fine." [I couldn't wait ten days if you paid me!]

"I'll look forward to it, Jill." And he told her where he would leave her ticket.

Needless to say, that was the end of the Scrabble game. One of her parents mildly questioned the logistics, and Jill quickly explained them away. "Oh, well, it would be a long way for him to come both before and after a game. Four trips to and from here. It's all right. Dad can take me, right?"

Pat agrees that maybe the setup was an example of his cockiness, at least his independence. He wasn't intentionally trying to be cold, but he admits he might not have tried such a cavalier move if the Bulls hadn't been such a success. Pat was a hit in Chicago, very visible. He thought a basketball game would excite Jill. In truth, a horseshoe match would have made her day if he was there. Pat had used the "choice of nights" technique he'd learned in the sales business. The idea was to put the emphasis on "which night" rather than on yes or no. Little did he know it was unnecessary. However, if for some reason Jill had been busy both those nights, no doubt she'd never have heard from him again.

From the time Jill got home from Bensenville after school

Friday until it was time for her and her dad to pull out of the driveway, she worked feverishly to look as sharp as she ever had. She wanted to leave nothing to chance.

The ticket was waiting at the will-call window, and if Jill had known basketball or the Chicago Stadium—which was located in one of the worst parts of town—she'd have realized what a great seat Pat had provided for her. It was a box right behind press row with a perfect view of the court. But an usher had to show her where it was. She had taken the ticket and slowly wandered into the arena, assuming Pat would be somewhere nearby, watching for her. But he wasn't. Finally she reached her seat and began casually scanning the stadium for him. She knew he was there, busily attending to something. But it was an enormous place with several levels, and it was filling up. The teams were warming up, and the game was about to begin. Still no Pat.

Finally, there he came. With little fanfare he shook her hand, told her he was glad she could make it and that it was nice to see her. "Wait right here after the game," he said.

It was a good thing he'd said that. She didn't have a plan B. Her father had driven back home, and as the game wound down, it was apparent the Bulls were going to lose a tough one to the Baltimore Bullets. The Bulls had led early and appeared to have the game well in hand. But the Bullets fought back and went ahead late in the last period, hanging on to win.

The stadium began to empty, and Jill worried about Pat's frame of mind. How were general managers supposed to take losses, especially one as difficult as this? Would he take it as hard as the coach and the players did? Or only as hard as the fans, who were disappointed but didn't make their livings trying to win basketball games?

Would he be angry? Quiet? In a bad mood? Would he want to go out at all or just want to drive her home? Maybe he'd rather she just found her own way home. She hadn't really thought about the outcome of the game until it happened. And again he was nowhere to be found. She didn't know he stood at one of the exits and thanked people for coming. It was his trademark but how did she know? She waited and waited, and soon she was the only person remaining in her section.

An usher came by, followed by a floor sweeper. "Starting to close up soon, ma'am," he said.

"I'm waiting for Pat Williams," she said.

"He knows you're here?"

"Yes."

"Okay."

In another twenty minutes some of the lights started to go out. And here he came. He didn't seem to be in a terrible mood, but it was clear he was suffering from the loss. He greeted the usher and the broom man by name, and it was apparent they revered him. "Want to get something to eat?" he asked her.

"That would be fine."

He took her to the Town and Country Restaurant off the Kennedy Expressway. With the social amenities out of the way, Pat fell silent and Jill felt the burden of the conversation fall on her. She had never considered herself an intellectual, and she knew too little about basketball, especially at the professional level, to attempt a foray there.

"My kids, my, uh, students, are so cute, Pat. You should meet them. They say the craziest things."

"Uh-huh."

"I love teaching."

"That's good. That's great, Jill."

"Some of the kids are from low-income families, you know."

"Are they?"

"Yes, and for me somehow that's more rewarding than teaching privileged children."

"Uh-huh."

Jill felt she could peer right through his forehead and see the replay of the game the Bulls had just lost. He ate a big meal so quickly that he finished appetizer, salad, entrée, and dessert before she had taken three bites of her sandwich. Most disconcerting was that he seemed to turn his chair to the side, not really facing her. The insecure little girl in her assumed he was pretending not to be with her, but to look as if he had just happened to be put there by the headwaiter.

Suddenly a man at the table behind Pat clapped him on the shoulder. "Hey, you Pat Williams of the Bulls?"

"Yes, sir," Pat said, turning.

"I'll tell you, this is something, meeting you tonight. You know, you gotta do something about security at the ticket windows. Look what I found here. Stacks of tickets somebody was sellin' or hawkin' or something."

"Hey, I appreciate that. We'll get on that. You've been very helpful."

On the way out Pat noticed Chicago Cub Don Kessinger and his newly acquired teammate Rick Monday. "Donnie, Rick," he said, "this is Jill Paige, a friend from the suburbs." But she had already decided he was embarrassed to be with her, that she had not been impressive, that indeed she had bored him and would not likely see him again. What she didn't know was that she was exactly right, at least on the last count.

Pat seemed to act as if he weren't really with her. She had to almost run to keep up with him, and he had come more alive talking with the man at the table behind him and with the Cubs than he had while listening to her talk about her class. He probably would have been the same with any woman. He was smarting from the loss, and yes, replaying the game in his mind. He was nervous and self-conscious and shy, in spite of the opposite image he wanted to portray.

Pat tried to act interested in her conversation. He wasn't put off by it, but he did have more exciting things happening in his life. He was in another world, a world of big names, fast action, and mega-buck deals. She knew that and couldn't hope to pretend to get in step immediately. It was what fascinated her about him, yet she couldn't discuss it, couldn't really relate to it. She was as attracted to him as she thought she'd be, if not more. But the evening, from her perspective, was a disaster. She had wished for and hoped for and expected so much more, maybe the big spark, maybe love at first sight, something, anything that would tell her she had won his attention.

By the time he drove her home, all she was hoping for was that somewhere along the line he would think enough of her to give her another chance. Down deep, she felt Pat had been a bit rude by being so quiet, but she kept fighting that feeling, not wanting it to surface full-blown. Her emotions were not ready for a bona fide negative thought about him yet. Her deepest fear was that he would think she was the reason for the lousy date. She knew she wasn't. At least she didn't feel she was, and she thought that if he were fair, he'd see that too. It was just a rocky start, that's all.

He drove her home, walked her to the door, shook her hand, said good night and thank you, and left. Jill told her mother, "He's so *nice, so* nice. I want to marry him." After *that* evening, she still wanted to marry him. If she had known what he was thinking, rather than just hoping against hope that he *wasn't* thinking it, she'd have cried herself to sleep.

From Pat's perspective, it was an awkward night. And he never gave a thought to whose fault it was. There was pain because of the basketball loss and the usual tension of two people, new to each other, trying to get in step with each other for the evening. "We parted," he recalls, "and as far as I was concerned, that was the end of it. I didn't come away thinking that this was it. I didn't have that feeling that, boy, I can't wait till next time. Nothing like that. It was nothing special. A pleasant enough evening, but we had lost. That had made it worse. Would I date her again? Nah, I didn't think so. My well-meaning Christian friends had fixed me up with some disasters, and this hadn't been that bad. It was a nice night and I was glad I went out with her, but life goes on. She obviously wasn't going to be the one."

Chapter Four

Self-Image

Who was this Pat Williams who had already decided that Jill Paige wasn't the one for him? At thirty-two he was the youngest general manager in professional sports. He was an easterner with a background in baseball, and an enigma to many people.

Pat was born in 1940 and grew up in Wilmington, Delaware, the only son in the family. His father was a football and baseball coach at Tower Hill, a private prep school, and wanted more than anything to see Pat become a professional athlete. Pat got a baseball glove for his third birthday and saw his first big-league baseball game in Philadelphia when he was seven.

It seemed his whole life was sports. He even played catch with his mother if there was no one else around. He followed his favorite teams and players like any other obsessive youngster, but he never grew out of it. He knew the records, the scores, the standings, the averages, all the statistics. His wall was covered with photos of players, and his earliest reading memories are of the sports pages in the Philadelphia papers.

His family wasn't wealthy, but because his father taught and coached at the private school, Pat was able to attend there. He quarterbacked the football team, played basketball, and was catcher on the baseball team. The star pitcher was his best friend, Ruly Carpenter, son of the owner of the Philadelphia Phillies National League baseball team. Pat and Ruly often went to spring training with the Phillies in Florida.

Pat's sisters teased him about girls and girlfriends, and of course, having a girlfriend when you were an athlete was cause for ridicule among your peers. So, despite his good looks and abilities, Pat hardly dated, and he was not comfortable when he did. He'd just as soon spend the weekend going to basketball games with his friends or playing ball himself.

While his sisters went to Vassar, Pat attended Wake Forest University on a baseball scholarship and was first-string catcher on a team that nearly went to the national NCAA finals in 1962. Pat's father was so proud of him that he would drive all night if necessary to attend as many games as possible. Pat was embarrassed that his father was always there, always cheering, always supportive. The other guys' fathers had seemed to grow out of that kind of interest as the boys got older, but Jim Williams was always Pat's biggest fan. Once he brought Popsicles to the game for everyone on Pat's team, and Pat suffered with the nickname "Popsicle" for the next several weeks.

When Mr. Williams tried to console his son after Wake Forest lost a game to Florida State that would have put them into the national tournament, Pat all but brushed him aside. He just wasn't in the mood for it and told his father he'd see him later. His college days were over, the Wake Forest baseball hopes had been dashed, and he just wanted to wind down and enjoy the leisurely ride home to Delaware with the guys. He never saw his father again.

When Pat finally arrived in Wilmington, his mother was waiting with the news that his father had been killed in an accident on the way home. Pat was so stunned, so remorseful over his last conversation with his dad, so appreciative of the love he had received and been embarrassed over, that it took him a long time to recover from the loss. Years later, he would still become emotional talking about his father.

Pat had hoped to be discovered by a major-league baseball team and get his career started, but the only offer he received was from Ruly Carpenter's dad. Mr. Carpenter offered to send him to the Phillies' class-D minor-league team in Florida and came through with a small bonus—so small, Pat quips, that it was easy to obey his instruction to not tell anyone about it. "Don't worry, sir," Pat says he told him. "I'm as embarrassed about this as you are."

Pat may have been good enough for class-D ball, but he also realizes that that break may simply have been Mr. Carpenter's way of helping out his son's best friend at a time of sorrow and need. Pat started strong in Florida, but it quickly became evident that he wasn't cut out for professional baseball. The experience became the grist for some of his best humor over the ensuing years.

Ferguson Jenkins, who went on to become a great pitcher, told people Pat was the toughest guy in the league to pitch to. "And he was my catcher!"

Pat says scouting reports on him to the home office said, "He may not be big, but he's slow."

Another assessment was that he was "in the twilight of a very mediocre career."

As disappointing as that realization was to Pat, the upshot was that he was invited to join the front office of the Phillies' minor-league team in Miami in 1964 to help in promotions and business, and learn to run the office. There were some early failures. He found it difficult to sell advertising pages in the program with his approach, "You wouldn't want to support the team by buying an ad, would you?" But when he learned to sell with the conviction that he was offering the best deal in town, his career started to turn.

He proved to be a natural in special promotions. He had enjoyed organizing big sporting events at Wake Forest, but he never dreamed how much he would love the business side of baseball. In the off-seasons he earned his master's degree at Indiana University and was a sportscaster, but his big break came in 1965 when the Phillies sent him to South Carolina to be president and general manager of the Spartanburg Phillies.

There he worked for a quiet southern gentleman, Mr. R. E. Littlejohn, who owned the ball club. Everyone called him Mr. R. E., and his quiet Christian example made a deep impact on Pat's life. The field manager of the Spartanburg team one year was former big leaguer Bobby Malkmus, an outspoken Christian. One of the first acts Pat booked to help boost attendance was Paul Anderson, the world's strongest man. After Anderson had amazed the crowd, and Pat, with his incredible feats of strength, he asked, "If I, the strongest man in the world, can't get through a day without Jesus Christ, what about you?"

Pat was active in the local chapter of the Fellowship of Christian Athletes (FCA), and soon all these various Christian influences began working on him. Meanwhile, his management and promotion abilities were earning him a reputation as a Bill Veeck protégé. Veeck, legendary owner of several big-league teams over the years, believed that short of a winning ball team, the best way to fill a stadium was to be sure the fans were treated like kings and queens, had fun, and were entertained. And he stopped at nothing to make sure of that. And so did Pat. He counts his conversations with Bill Veeck back then among the highlights of his life.

The team was winning, the stands were full, Pat was setting and reaching goal after goal. He was committed to excellence, to doing whatever was necessary to ensure success for himself and the organization. When he became bitterly disappointed at not being named minor-league executive of 1966 by the *Sporting News,* it became obvious that Pat Williams was living only for Pat Williams.

Everything was dedicated to career goals. Climbing the ladder. His Mecca was the big-league club. If he did his job, played his cards right, devoted every waking hour to the task, maybe someday he'd be general manager of the big-league Phillies. And his longtime friend Ruly would probably be owner and president by then.

But when the 1966 season was over, and the club had won the championship, and the attendance records had been broken and reset out of sight, Pat went home to his apartment with the Peggy Lee hit *Is That All There Is?* ringing in his ears.

Life was empty. Life was a lark. Life was a joke. Life was a tease. Nothing satisfied. He kept thinking that if he could just reach the next milestone, the next achievement, the next success, the next bit of notoriety, that would be all he needed. But they were all false gods. They all were sticks and carrots, leading him further and further down the road to frustration. At twenty-six he was feeling old, confused, defeated. If the success syndrome didn't have the answer to happiness and fulfillment, what did?

Pat's selfishness and cockiness even strained the relationship with his old friends, the Carpenters. In 1967 they asked him to take over the Reading, Pennsylvania, Phillies farm club that had floundered for years. He said no way, turned it down out of hand. Who wanted to go to some unknown and unproven town like that when he had everything going for him in Spartanburg?

It didn't take him long to realize that one doesn't enhance one's career by flying in the face of the bosses and turning down assignments and transfers. Despite all the successes he enjoyed, he still hadn't achieved the *Sporting News* honor he wanted, and he had created a rift between himself and his bosses—who were also some of his oldest friends—that would never really heal.

Then one night in 1968 he heard a Campus Crusade singing group who were visiting Spartanburg, and he was fascinated by how sharp and wholesome and happy and alive they seemed. He was also mystified by how easily and unabashedly they referred to Christ and the Lord and what He meant in their lives. They hung around to chat with people later, and Pat thought he'd try to get next to a cute blonde. He asked for a breakfast date and she accepted, assuming he was interested in spiritual things. By the time she got through with him the next morning, carefully explaining the *Four Spiritual Laws,* he was interested. He promised to think about what she'd said, as she and her friends boarded their bus and pulled out of sight toward the next town.

He knew he was onto something but he had never felt so lonely in his life. He went to see Mr. Littlejohn and told him what he'd heard and how it was affecting him. The old man quietly led him to Christ, praying with him as Pat confessed his

sins and told God he believed that Christ loved him enough to
die for him and wanted priority in his life.

Pat was changed, almost immediately, from the inside out.
His temper was under control, his self-centered motivation was
gone, his empty striving for notoriety was replaced with a desire to serve Christ. He spoke of his newfound faith everywhere
he went, and he became a person people loved to work with
and for.

He didn't let up at all in his total commitment to the fans
who supported the Spartanburg Phillies. He worked tirelessly
to bring them the best return for their entertainment dollar,
thrilling them with reasons to come to the ballpark, and maintaining a championship team too. When he was finally ready
for it, the honor was his of Executive of the Year for the previous minor league season.

When the invitation came in 1968 to become business manager of the Philadelphia 76ers, Pat thought long and hard
about changing sports. He had always loved basketball, and
there was some magic associated with the smaller arena, the
indoor feel, the new challenge. He prayed about it and decided
that if he was ever going to make a major change, now was the
time. It wasn't a general managership, but it was a start.

And he made the most of it. After an impressive first year, he
was interviewed by the new owners of the Chicago Bulls, still a
young entry in the National Basketball Association. They offered him the job as general manager, and Pat jumped at the
chance. He would be in charge of an NBA team in the third
largest market in the country, and at twenty-nine, the youngest
general manager in the history of professional sports.

His work was cut out for him. Chicago was a baseball and
football town and hadn't seen a championship in either sport
since the Bears won the National Football League title in 1963.
The White Sox had gone to the baseball World Series in 1959
but lost to the Dodgers, and the last time the Cubs had been in
the series, they lost, in 1945.

Pat decided to take the Bulls by the horns. He rented a nice
apartment not far from the club office in the Sheraton Chicago
Hotel, settled into Moody Church as his new house of worship,

under the ministry of Pastor George Sweeting, became active in the local FCA chapter, and threw himself into both building an exciting basketball team and informing an apathetic Chicago public about it.

Friends were always trying to arrange blind dates for him, but most often these were disappointing failures. He really wanted to discover someone on his own, if that's what God wanted for him. If only there was time and the opportunity to think about it.

He took any and every speaking engagement that came along, never passing up an opportunity to turn the crowd on with his dry humor and then whet their appetites for an evening at a Bulls game. Average attendance doubled overnight as Pat brought in half-time shows and special promotions that made the games attractive, while the Bulls were becoming serious contenders for the NBA crown.

It wasn't unusual for him to speak nearly three hundred times a year, and regardless of the setting or audience, he also made sure he spoke of his faith in Christ. He wasn't growing spiritually in his personal development, except for the good Bible preaching he heard when he was in town on Sundays. There was little time for personal devotions—at least he hadn't made them a priority—and except for a few opportunities with the FCA, he wasn't sharing his faith on a one-to-one basis either. But he was in great demand as a speaker.

And so it was by Thanksgiving of 1971 that he had been in town two years, was solidly entrenched as the media's favorite Most Eligible Bachelor, and had been invited to speak at his own church for a special evening lined up by the new pastor. George Sweeting had become president of the Moody Bible Institute, and Warren Wiersbe was the new man at Moody Church. Pat was excited about the evening.

Long before he had become a Christian, Pat Williams had been indoctrinated with the Veeckian philosophy that wherever two or three are gathered together, you join them for a hand of bridge and sell them on your product. He had always believed that the only way to interest people in professional basketball was to just go out and sell it. So, while he was sharing his faith at civic functions where his main purpose was to sell basketball, he also sold basketball at Christian speaking engagements where his main purpose was to share his faith.

Mr. Littlejohn had convinced Pat that his speaking ability was a spiritual gift and that he should use it every chance he could. "You can be an example and an influence," his former boss had said. And so even though he wasn't growing as a Christian, he still had the desire to exercise his gift. People were asking to hear his testimony, and he was happy to tell it.

Pat had been honored and flattered when Pastor Wiersbe asked him to speak at the Frank Boggs Thanksgiving concert. He spent much of the day at the home of Bulls coach, Dick Motta, in Northbrook, enjoying Thanksgiving dinner with the Motta family. When he got down to Moody Church that evening, he could hardly believe the crowd. "The place was just busting," he recalls. "It was an awesome, exciting sight, and I knew it would be an upbeat evening. I felt comfortable speaking, and it was an emotional high just to be on the same program with Frank Boggs. Afterward I had been invited to go out for dessert with some of the people from the church staff, and I looked forward to that as the perfect capper for the evening."

As for his encounter with Jill Paige, he remembers the words *striking* and *attractive* and *poised* going through his mind. Asking for her phone number was something he'd never done with anyone before. But she had opened the door by asking about his speaking to her students, and he stepped through, thinking he'd really been smooth. As she walked away, he folded the name and number and put it in his pocket thinking, *Not too bad, Williams. It's a start.* "In fact," he says now, "I thought I had accomplished something of major proportions. Not that I was particularly interested in this girl. How could I be yet? But it was a big step for me just to be arranging something for myself on my own, and I was a little proud of myself. Of course, at that point I had no idea that she had engineered the whole thing."

Chapter Five

Courtship

If Jill thought the wait between the first call and the first date was miserable, she really suffered waiting for another contact from Pat. In fact, he had reacted to her conversation just the way she feared, and had she known that, she probably would have given up on him.

As a gesture of kindness, Pat jotted Jill a note. She tore it open. "Dear Jill, I was impressed. Pat."

"I was impressed?" she repeated. "I'm not interested in 'impressed.' I'm looking for 'madly in love with.' Or at least, 'Thanks for the date.' "

Jill waited another excruciating month, then decided to take things into her own hands. She had her dad drive her to Chicago Stadium on a Sunday afternoon in February, sit with her through the Bulls game, then wait in the car while she tried to just happen to run into Pat. Which she did.

"I just wanted to say hi," she said, "and see how you were doing." Pat admits that it was how absolutely gorgeous she looked that made him think it would be nice to have her join him that evening for a big Fellowship of Christian Athletes rally in Evanston. Several top names in Chicago sports would be there and it promised to be a great evening. So much the better to have a beautiful girl with him. It would be fun.

And it was. Sort of. Again, it was not a smooth, enjoyable evening. Still a little awkward. Nothing special. Except for Jill. Jill was in heaven. Pat was in Chicago.

Sometime during the evening Pat idly assured her that he'd be happy to leave tickets for her and her father occasionally. A few times she took advantage of that, but rarely did she see Pat at the games. "He never sought me out. I told myself he was too busy. Sometimes I'd see him later at the door, and once in a great while he'd ask me out. Very infrequently."

Pat sent her an Easter lily which so encouraged her that she called to thank him from Kansas where she was visiting friends. That almost made him regret it. He hadn't meant to say that much with the gesture. He just knew she was a sharp Christian girl and that she'd probably get a kick out of it. "The fact is," she says now, "Pat wasn't shrewd enough then to be playing games with me. It might have seemed so to me at the time if I had known what he was thinking, but I didn't. And now I know he wouldn't have done it with a bad motive."

Soon it became obvious to Pat that he was being chased. He would invite Jill out after a game because she was there and she looked good and her dad was in the car and Pat felt a little obligated. Then she'd just happen to show up at Moody Church and he had to deal with her there. He wasn't about to take her out every time she appeared, and it was clear now from the way she glowed when she saw him that she had fallen for him.

Part of Pat was flattered, but he felt nothing for her. They had been out a few times and he had not been smitten. She had even called him at the office a few times, and that was all right, but . . .

One Sunday night at Moody Church, just before the closing prayer, he was sitting back down after a hymn and caught sight of her out of the corner of his eye. *Oh, no! Now what do I do?* During the prayer he ducked out. She couldn't figure out where he'd disappeared to.

The next time, she kept an eye on him during the benediction and saw him hustle out. Could it be that he was avoiding her? She didn't want to think about it. It would have broken her heart. But just in case, she quit calling, quit trying to run into him, quit following him during Bulls games with her binoculars from the third balcony ("Absolutely true," she confesses). After games where she had never even run into him, she was satisfied simply to have been in the same general area with him for a few hours. "That was almost enough," she says. "Just to see him from a distance. I would rather he was deeply in love with me and would tell me so, yes. The words 'I love you' were not expressed much around our house, even though we all loved each other. My parents weren't big on telling each other, at least in front of me, and I didn't tell them either, even though they knew. But I dreamed of being told that by the man I loved. Of course, I was loving a man I didn't really know, but logic was irrelevant at that point."

When she had had all the silence she could stand, she wanted to give him one more chance. She called about getting tickets, and he seemed to be more cordial over the phone. Easier to talk to. Less awkward. She actually enjoyed it. The next game she went to resulted in dinner afterward. Still no fireworks, but all of a sudden he would call her occasionally. "I guess I just realized that she was too nice to be afraid of. She was so well-mannered and obviously a classy girl, I started to enjoy chatting with her on the phone. I protected myself, however, by not limiting my dating activity to her. There were others, none serious. That's how I viewed Jill. She could be one of the few now that she didn't scare me so much."

The more they talked by phone, the more Pat enjoyed it and the more he initiated it. The conversations got longer and longer, but Pat still wanted to be in control when they saw each other and when they went out.

A big turning point came in mid-June when Jill told him she had won the Miss Western Cook County Pageant and would be in the Miss Illinois competition in Aurora in July. What really impressed Pat was the fact that she had done this without telling him in advance. It was all said and done when he heard about it, and he thought, *Well, now, maybe I do have something here!* "I know how terrible that sounds," he says, "but it's the truth. She had my attention and I started more seriously looking into the potential there."

The news of the pageant resulted in longer phone calls. "I was fascinated with the competition part. That really got to me. Finally, something we could share. It may have been talent and looks and musical ability as opposed to passing and shooting and running and defense, but it was competition, and *that* I was interested in. I wanted to know all about it. What did it mean? How did it work? What did she have to do? How did they judge it? What was her talent? Violin? Oh, very impressive. Big time. What happens next? Keep me posted. I was really getting into it. Maybe this was more than just one of the girls I dated and called occasionally."

But when she asked if he would come and cheer for her at the Miss Illinois Pageant the following month, he said, "I don't know. Maybe. July is an awfully busy month." For pro basketball? She knew better than that. She detected his defense mechanisms going up.

And she still wasn't his first choice for dates. He had been invited to speak July 3 at a Billy Graham crusade on the other side of Illinois, and it meant a three-hour drive each way. He thought it would be nice to share the trip with a fun, good-looking girl. Jill? Nope. A stewardess he had dated a few times. Too bad. She would be in New Orleans that day. *Maybe I'll call Jill.*

She just happened to be free that day, and sure, she'd be happy to ride along. They'd go in the afternoon, he'd give his talk, and they'd come back late that night. For some reason, from the moment he picked her up that afternoon until she found them a Denny's restaurant near the high school where he was supposed to speak—she knew the area because her sister was going to Augustana College nearby—they were more relaxed with each other than they had ever been. They had dated no more than once a month since January, yet this was the first time both felt comfortable. By the time they sat eating dinner, Pat had lost his tension over the speaking he had to do that evening.

But it was after his obligation was over, when there was nothing left to do but enjoy the drive back to Chicago and find a place to have a late snack, that Pat really let his hair down. It was a unique experience for him. He had never remembered acting so natural in front of a girl, so like himself. All his dates had been awkward, almost formal, affairs, and he'd dated only a few women more than twice. Either he lost interest or they became unavailable. Here was someone who was obviously interested in him. He felt comfortable with her, and that freed him to act a little crazy.

They laughed and sang and joked and squealed. He made up poems and songs and changed the words to songs on the radio. He imagined conversations with people they saw walking by. He couldn't believe himself. She laughed till she cried. But the bottom line in her mind was that he finally seemed to have had a good time with her. She had *always* had a good time with him. That was easy. Even when she knew he was bored and she was desperate to liven things up, she was satisfied. She enjoyed being with him and only wished he would enjoy it too. Well, now he was, and she was thrilled. They still hadn't held hands. She hadn't felt bold enough to gaze into his eyes—at least when he was looking—and of course, nothing had been expressed, serious or kidding, about them as a couple, a pair, a thing, an item.

But the trip had been a turning point, and they both knew it. "It was absolutely unbelievable," Pat says. "I clowned around and she seemed looser too. It was a revelation to me. I had never known I could have that much fun with a woman. Nothing had clicked with her before, and I'm not saying I had fallen in love yet, but to me it was a very significant evening."

That was an understatement. Pat woke up the next morning with Jill on his mind. He might even have called to see if she was free that evening, but a Bulls scout, Jerry Krause, called to ask if Pat wanted to go to the White Sox game. Pat was always up for a good ball game. The day seemed to move slowly, even for a Fourth of July, but Pat thought it was just because he was looking forward to seeing the Sox. It was athletic events that had interrupted his short-lived high school and college romances. If the girls didn't want to go to the games and tournaments, then they'd just have to wait until he got back. And none would.

It was a frigid night at the ball park—only in Chicago in July!—but that wasn't the reason Pat couldn't keep his mind on the game. Talk about unique. The world's most obsessive sports fan was strangely uninterested. His mind was on Jill. He knew he was getting serious. He couldn't help wondering, *What if she wins it? I'll be dating Miss Illinois! Pretty heavy stuff.*

Jill had good motives for wanting to be Miss America. She admits she entered the Miss Western Cook County competition "because of pageant fever. I liked being in them. I liked the competition and the attention. But I really wanted to be Miss America for a bigger reason, and as hokey as it may sound, I was serious about it. I wanted to use the platform I would have as Miss America to speak out for my faith. That was my true, underlying goal, and whatever God wanted for me, knowing my heart, was all right with me. I did not enter these pageants in the hope that Pat would be impressed. In fact, I'd rather he'd have fallen for me before he knew about all of that." But he didn't. There's no getting around it. It embarrasses Pat that it took that kind of public recognition for Jill before he took notice, but that's the way it was.

The girls were sequestered at the pageant, so the only contact Pat could have with her was by messenger. Maybe it was that absence or the inaccessibility, but something made him send daily telegrams, letters, flowers, notes, everything. And yes, he showed up for the preliminary competition every night, driving all the way out from Chicago. All of a sudden, she was a priority.

"Still, I wasn't ready to say I was in love with her. But the signs were sure there. I was tremendously interested, let's say that. We were clicking. I was absorbed with her, absolutely, totally enamored with her. I was into what she was doing, where she was, how she was feeling. I wanted to know everything. I was preoccupied the whole day, excited about her."

For years Pat had wondered how he would find a life's partner. He knew dating and relationships with women were his weak areas. He didn't know all the reasons, but he knew that had been a problem. He had prayed that God would simply make His choice clear to Pat, then make it all happen. He knew it would likely be someone younger than he, someone committed to Christ, someone with class and dignity. But how it would happen, he simply didn't know. *Maybe,* he thought, *this is it.* But he wasn't going to jump to any conclusions.

For four straight nights, Pat was in the audience by himself. Jill's parents were there too, of course, but he wasn't ready to sit with them, for fear of what that might imply. Some nights he simply left when the show was over. Other times he stayed around and tried to at least make eye contact with Jill, wave, or something. All week he took in the pageant like a sporting event, scouting and judging each contestant on his own.

At first he wondered if he was too biased, because he had Jill winning everything. He didn't have to wonder if she was the crowd's favorite. That was obvious. She won the bathing-suit competition and scored very high in talent. She was radiant, easily the best-looking girl among the dozens vying for the title. By the last night, Pat was sure she had it wrapped up. So, it seemed, did almost everyone else.

On Saturday, the big night, Pat finally sat with Mr. and Mrs. Paige. His program was dog-eared and scribbled up by now, and some of the comments he had written about the other contestants would have been embarrassing to the Paiges. But he was proud of himself for having agreed with the judges almost perfectly on the final ten.

The finalists went through the three phases of the competition for the second time that week. It was as exciting as any game, and he was ready to explode. The Paiges appeared serene. They had coached Jill from the first pageant she ever entered to just accept the Lord's will. And that's what she wanted to do. Jill wasn't sure about her own chances. She knew the crowd was hers—almost embarrassingly so. Any time she was announced, ovations and cheers shook the auditorium. Pat was certain it was all over but the shouting.

The fourth, third, and second runners-up were named and their prizes and scholarships announced. Now it was just down to Jill and one other. Pat leaned over to Mrs. Paige and, surprising even himself, said, "We've got it, Mom."

Pat wondered what it would all mean, going with Miss Illinois, waiting a year while she served in that capacity, following her to Atlantic City for the Miss America Pageant—he couldn't even allow himself to consider whether she might win that; this was enough. On stage, Jill was exhilarated at being so close to winning. She breathed a sincere prayer: "Lord, whatever you want for me is perfectly fine."

The beautiful emcee, former Miss America Phyllis George, now of CBS television, walked to the microphone and calmly pulled a sheet of paper from a sealed envelope. "And now, ladies and gentlemen, the moment we have all been waiting for. The first runner-up in the 1972 Miss Illinois pageant is . . . Miss Western Cook County, Jill Marie Paige!"

Chapter Six

Preparing for Marriage

Pat was furious. The crowd was stunned. There was a full two-second pause to let it sink in, and then, during the celebration for the new Miss Illinois, Pat kicked the chair ahead of him and slammed his program to the floor. There was enough noise and the Paiges were applauding loudly enough that his tirade went unnoticed, but he remained in a funk for a couple of hours. To this day he believes the decision was a poor one, but at the time Jill wouldn't hear of it.

She had meant the prayer she had offered just seconds before, and while she would have her moments later wondering "what if" and "why not," she was satisfied that God's will had been done. She was thrilled to have finished first runner-up, and she was puzzled at Pat's reaction. She was glad he'd been in her corner, but rather than being happy with second place, he fumed that she had "lost."

Jill hurried around, congratulating all the other girls and consoling her family and other supporters. At the post-pageant reception Pat sulked, sitting there with a long face, but he was amazed at how Jill handled herself. He began to wonder now if his relationship with her would end the way it had with the girl at Wake Forest—if she would suddenly lose interest just as he was getting in the game. He knew it appeared that her new prominence had caught his attention, but if that was what it took for God to wake him up to the girl meant for him, what was wrong with that?

Finally he could be with her again. She had responsibilities
and was still chatting with friends, but she was "with" him, and
every chance she got she looked into his eyes and thanked him
for coming and being so concerned. And she told him it was all
right; she didn't feel as if she'd lost. It wasn't like finishing in
second place in a big basketball tournament where winning is
all that matters. It was more like finishing in the top two in a
scholarship, beauty, and poise competition, and she was
happy.

She made it very clear to Pat that it was important to her
that he join her at the final brunch the next morning where the
trophies would be presented. They embraced, they kissed, they
held hands. This was new to him. This could have been the
time for her to say, hey, it's been fun, big guy, but I have a lot
of things to do and people to see and quite a full social calendar. Now it was Pat who was worried about what Jill thought
and how she would react. It was his turn to worry about where
he stood with her. And now he had found out. "I'll be here," he
promised. "And I'll take you back to Riverside too."

That evening in his apartment Pat was able to lay to rest the
feeling of injustice he had harbored since the pageant judges'
decision had been announced. It was unfair, a no-brainer as he
liked to say, but it was over and nothing could be done about
it. He was so high from his quickly blossoming relationship
with Jill that he could hardly concentrate on anything else.
Sleep was elusive. He just wanted to see her again.

He was up earlier than he needed to be, but there was no
sense tossing and turning. He flipped on the radio and listened
to Billy Graham's *The Hour of Decision,* a title which was more
meaningful for him than he realized. Of course, Pat's mind was
on Jill as he shaved and listened to George Beverly Shea sing
I'd Rather Have Jesus.

As he hummed along, only slightly aware of the words—
than silver or gold; I'd rather be His than have riches untold—he
was suddenly overcome with emotion. In that steamy bathroom, standing before the mirror, half his face still covered
with lather, Pat broke down. It seemed to him that God was

breaking into his life and heart and soul with the message that he was to marry this girl. To him it was "clear as a bell, more a discovery than a decision."

"So few decisions in my life—since I had become a Christian—were really decisions. It was more as if God just opened the door and I walked through. And now here He was again, opening another door. The whole thing, the relationship, was so bizarre. The times I assumed it was over, the times I was aware of her pursuit and ran from it, the times I was afraid it was over and didn't want it to be. And now this."

Pat was nervous, edgy, eager to race back to Aurora for the brunch. Jill greeted him warmly, and he knew he was in love. It was dawning on him that *she* had been for some time. Again he was proud of her as she played the difficult role of number two, accepting the second-to-last trophy presented and enjoying the warm applause of the other contestants and their families and friends. Mr. and Mrs. Paige beamed as they congratulated her and saw that both Pat and Jill were really beginning to enjoy each other's company.

When it was all over, Pat helped Jill pack her belongings in his car, they bade good-bye to her parents, and set off for home. She had tossed her trophy on top of everything else in the backseat. She sat close to Pat and breathed deeply, relieved that it was all over. "I still think you were number one," he said. And they chatted about how hectic her life would have been if she *had* won the top prize. "We probably would have seen very little of each other for the next year," she said.

Pat said he wouldn't have liked that and Jill smiled at him. Somewhere up the road, north and east of Aurora, Pat said, "Well, I guess we'll end up getting married."

Jill was stunned, she wanted to scream, to jump around, to throw her arms around him and plaster him with a warm kiss. But she felt the strange need to keep her cool, maintain her poker face, not act too excited. Maybe if she reacted too overtly it would vanish, fade away like some bad joke. She was thinking, *It's about time!* but she was also praying he was serious and wouldn't change his mind.

"There's someone I want you to meet," Pat said. "One of my best friends. He and his wife have meant a lot to me since I've been in Chicago. His place is on the way." He introduced Jill to Norm and Carole Sonju, a couple who had taken Pat under their wings and had fixed him up with a few girls they thought would be right for him. He was eager to show off his own discovery and to see what they thought of Jill.

The Sonjus seemed very nice, but it was all a little puzzling to Jill. Pat went on and on about her being first runner-up, winning the bathing-suit competition, and all that. Jill just listened and didn't say much. She didn't know that Pat was running her by for his best friend's approval. Norm would later be best man in the wedding, and it was important to Pat to get his reaction. The trouble was, he didn't tell Norm that's what he wanted. He decided to just wait until Norm called him, and he vowed to himself that he wouldn't call Norm for the rest of his life unless Norm called first.

A few days later, on the night of the 1972 all-star baseball game, Norm Sonju called. He had decided that if Pat could be dragged away from television to talk about Jill, then it was serious. Pat was thinking that if Norm could drag himself away from his TV, he must have been impressed. He was.

He raved about Jill. How humble she was. How quiet. How she'd left her trophy in the car, and that when they walked Pat and Jill to the car he saw it casually tossed into the backseat. He and Carole liked that. She was beautiful, perfect, and had their blessing. Pat was happy. God had impressed his decision on him the morning before he semiproposed, but for some reason he felt the need for confirmation from Norm. It was important to Pat, and it made him even more excited. If Jill had known he was waiting for that, she would have been crushed. She didn't know until after they were married, and then she teased him about what might have happened if God had approved and Norm hadn't. "Which way would you have leaned, Ace?"

Pat quickly became the organizer. "So, Jill, how do we get this done? What happens next?"

"Well," she said, "you start by getting me a ring. Surprise me. As long as the diamond is oval shaped, I'll be thrilled. Then we have to get a license, physicals, blood tests, and arrange for the church, a florist, my dress, a restaurant for the rehearsal and reception dinners, music, the ministers, that kind of thing."

"And if either of us fails the physical?"

She feared he was serious. *Would this turkey call the whole thing off?* Much of his life was wrapped up in making no-cut deals with players who had to pass their physicals.

By the time of the rehearsal, everything was in place. Pat called the Wheaton Police Department to request help the next day with the traffic. When asked who was calling, he said, "The bride." Not too nervous.

When Jill was an hour late to the rehearsal, basically because the wet weather caused her sister to have trouble styling Jill's hair, Pat took unmerciful ribbing from his attendants. They had him convinced he'd been jilted. They were teasing, but he sincerely felt his worst fear was coming to pass. He almost wept when she arrived.

Bad weather on their October wedding day may have "hurt the crowd," in Pat's vernacular, but still, more than fifteen hundred showed up. Pat's cousin, David Parsons, and Jill's sister and mother all took part in the music along with the Melody Four Quartet lead singer Glenn Jorian. Pat's uncle, the Reverend R. Murphy Williams, and Dr. Warren Wiersbe officiated.

Pat felt as if he'd been running a mile a minute since the Miss Illinois Pageant. When he finally stood at the front of the church with his bride, he was forced to slow down, to stop for the first time in months. Suddenly he was overwhelmed with the moment. It was so right, so perfect, so God ordained. He was proud and pleased and knew exactly what it all meant. It was the most emotional moment in his life, and he began to shudder. He didn't just tremble, he shook uncontrollably. He felt he had lost control of his legs and was afraid he was going to faint.

Jill feared the same. She had sat through many weddings for

which her mother played the organ, and they had seen more than one groom just drop to the floor. R. E. Littlejohn, sitting near the front, had decided that if Pat didn't quit shaking within thirty seconds, "I was goin' up there to get him."

But Pat wasn't in trouble. "I knew I wasn't afraid. It was just overwhelming. I felt great; now if I could just stay upright."

The problem was, Pat couldn't communicate that to Jill, who was getting angry at him "for ruining my wedding. I was thinking, *If anything happens, I'll kill him.*" Somehow, Pat made it through, and then they were off to the Holiday Inn in Glen Ellyn for the reception dinner for two hundred.

Jill had planned that too and was in her glory. She was at her best when organizing things, and she enjoyed nothing better than seeing those plans come to fruition. By the end of it, though, she became very aware of the fact that she had pretty much done it all and Pat had simply shown up to take part. Not that she wasn't glad he was there ... But when it came time to get to O'Hare Airport for the surprise honeymoon trip, Pat was off somewhere talking with Mr. Littlejohn. He had already been counseled by long-distance telephone by Mrs. Littlejohn over the past several months. When he asked her how one knew one was in love, she asked a few questions and said, "You are."

But now Jill even had to get their things down to the lobby for the ride to the airport. And they were going to be late for their ten o'clock flight. No problem, Pat assured her. He had already assumed that and had Norm call ahead to hold the plane. That was impressive, but she wanted help in the little things, the mundane things, like the luggage. She lapsed into her first silent treament.

"What's wrong?"

"Nothing."

"You sure?"

"Yes, nothing."

He was puzzled. He had spent a lot of time saying good-bye to out-of-town guests, thanking them for coming, and apparently she had wanted him by her side when she was changing and getting ready to leave. It was something new to him, seeing her that upset. But he couldn't get out of her exactly what he had done wrong. It would be days before she brought up this first offense.

On the plane the pilot welcomed the new Mr. and Mrs. Pat Williams and explained the delay to the rest of the passengers. Jill didn't know where they were going until the next morning, after they'd spent the night in New York and then boarded another flight to Aruba. She'd heard of it, but knew nothing about it.

Aruba, fifteen miles from South America and thirty from the equator, is a quaint, Dutch-flavored island in the Netherlands Antilles. It was beautiful, and they stayed in a nice hotel, finding some day tours to occupy their time. Jill had wanted to sunbathe the time away, but Pat badly burned his neck and the tops of his feet jogging on the beach the first morning.

There was no stepping out to the pool either. The travel agency had not informed Pat that it was under repair, so their poolside room put them in a perfect spot to hear jackhammers all day. When Pat did try to spend time with Jill on the beach, he wore a Bulls warm-up shirt, maroon shorts, and knee-high black dress socks. She would rather he had stayed inside.

Pat went through a painful withdrawal from his world of radio and TV news and newspapers and magazines. He was frustrated and edgy. Jill wanted him to lie with her on the beach and tell her she was his lifelong dream come true. Pat wanted to jog and find out what was happening in the World Series; and he could do neither.

What a relief when he spotted a copy of the international edition of the *New York Times!* He pored over it the way a man dying of thirst would go after a fresh mountain spring. Jill couldn't believe it. Then, when he first saw that the hotel on the other end of the beach posted teletype printouts of news and scores from the States, he thought it was a mirage!

Every evening after dinner they hiked down the beach so he could catch up on the news and sports. He was having a fine time. It wasn't exactly what Jill had dreamed of. Pat noticed a few of her little "hurt treatments" as he called them, and worried some that she might not understand the way a professional sports person immerses himself in the whole sports scene.

She worried that she would never understand a man who was obsessed with sports even on his honeymoon. There was probably room for some compromise on both sides, but Jill knew what she wanted and realized she might have to mold this man to fit it. Was he moldable? He told her plainly that he couldn't see her getting upset at his wanting to read a few scores. What he didn't know was that he was to be on the receiving end of a lot of similar pouting sessions as the years rolled on.

"In retrospect," he says, "we really didn't know each other. We had this whirlwind thing that had been triggered that summer, and I was caught up in all her talent and success. I just hoped she understood what I was into. Because when we got back to our new little apartment in Chicago, it would be right back into the full-time, full-speed world of the NBA. I would have to hit the ground running and I wouldn't be letting up until the season was over."

In fact, there was more waiting in Chicago for Pat than he knew. His secure world with the Bulls was about to crumble under the new ownership, and it would be a bitter, painful ordeal for him. He had not really suffered a failure since he had become a Christian, and without having spent undue time in his Bible, he thought maybe that was part of the package: You love God, God loves you, and you're taken care of. No hassles, no burdens, no trials. Trouble was ahead.

And would he be able to tell his life's companion? How could he? What would she think? He had it all together. She had married an image of success, of macho, of a man who handled everything. He would have to keep the details from her, work out his own plan of escape, and make it all look natural.

Chapter Seven

Adjustment

Jill's teaching assignment had changed that September, and rather than having her own class all day, she was teaching music to all the classes. "Music class became the time for students to mess around," she says, "and I quickly got tired of it." Trying, in addition, to make it to every Bulls home game and then driving all the way to Bensenville the next morning was taking its toll.

She was unaware of the hotbed of controversy to which Pat had returned. The friendly owners who'd hired him in 1969 and whom he'd so enjoyed working for had sold the club, and the new owners were bottom-line specialists who didn't always side with their general manager.

Pat had been enormously successful for almost ten years, the last four in basketball and the last three in Chicago, but now his star was on the wane. He kept it from almost everyone, especially Jill. He simply didn't know her well enough to know how she would take it. Why worry her? Why let her wonder about his ability or security?

Meanwhile, Jill was enjoying being a wife. Pat went with her to shop for the first few pieces of furniture, but it wasn't long before he realized that wasn't his scene. He assured Jill that he trusted her and believed in her and admired her taste in furniture, so however she wanted to furnish the apartment was fine with him.

Jill vacillated between being flattered and feeling neglected when she had furniture delivered that Pat hadn't seen yet. He always seemed to like it, but she couldn't tell whether that was because he was relieved by not having to participate in the buying or because she really was a super interior decorator.

Shortly, Pat asked Jill if she would handle the money. He'd give her his check, she'd deposit it along with hers, and she would pay all the bills and monitor the budget. In her family, her father had handled that, so she had grown up thinking that was the way it was supposed to be. She agreed to do it, however, but felt very put upon.

It was fortunate that Jill was good with the money, because Pat never asked how it was going. Only occasionally did one of them make a major purchase without checking with the other, and then have to limp until payday. But Pat was being paid handsomely, and with Jill's income as well they had few financial worries.

Through the years, Jill came to appreciate her financial freedom, because she met many wives who felt they couldn't spend a dollar unless it was all right with their husbands. "If it had to be one way or the other, I preferred it the way I had it. Of course, he knew I wouldn't abuse the privilege. And I learned that he was pretty frugal—that was kind; I kid him that he's really a cheapskate—so I'd just as soon have access to the checkbook."

The most difficult early adjustment Jill had to make was to Pat's schedule. He was involved at the office and on the phone until late into the night, and then on weekends he either watched football or basketball games on television, or he slept. Jill felt fortunate that he wasn't gone all day Saturday playing golf, but she was irritated that he was either in bed or in front of the television set. She forced herself to watch with him, not wanting to be a TV sports widow. "He was the first man who was ever able to explain football to me so I could understand it."

As fall 1972 passed and Christmas approached, their routine was predictable: "We ate dinner together, we went to church together, we went to bed together, and we got up in the morning and went our separate ways to work. I thought that's what being married was all about," Jill says.

She was thrilled to have married the man she wanted to marry, and she enjoyed the ego trip that went with his being recognized just about anywhere they went. Pat did seem terribly busy, too busy even for a man in his position, she thought. And there were times when she wondered if he had just gotten used to being that busy because he'd been single for so long and had nothing else to do. But now he was married and there were things she would like them to do together, but work came first.

It didn't seem that he was manufacturing reasons to be away from her—even if he'd sometimes done that before they were married. The dribs and drabs she heard about the work at the office made it sound very hectic and intense, and as she slowly learned about the world of professional sports, she realized it was a few people doing a lot of work for the enjoyment of thousands of fans. It was high pressure, and there was little margin for error. Had she been married to Pat during any of his first three years in Chicago, she would have been able to compare his moods then with the current year and know that something was different.

How could she know he wasn't enjoying his job anymore? He seemed to be immersed in it all the time. Games, calls, overnight trips, TV, papers, magazines; you name it, he was into it. His job and his interest in all sports permeated his life. It was hard to imagine someone being more committed to what he was doing, but she figured that was what made him what he was, put him where he was, and made him so attractive to her.

For some reason, Jill worried that Pat wouldn't have the time even to think about buying her any Christmas presents that year. Either she was taking a cue from his attitude toward furniture shopping, or she thought he would be too busy. She wasn't thinking that he wouldn't *want* to, just that he might not.

To protect herself, she bought a present, wrapped it, and put

"To Jill, Love Pat" on the card. She was a little chagrined on Christmas morning, after she had asked him if he wanted to see "what you bought me," when he had indeed bought her something.

In February, with Pat's permission, Jill quit teaching and became a full-time housewife. "As I think back on it—before children, of course—I don't know what I did with my time other than shop in the morning and watch soap operas in the afternoon, the things I speak against now. I'd give anything to have that wasted time back."

The Paiges had not had television in their home until Jill was almost twelve, and even then, her parents limited the viewing. There were a couple of shows the whole family enjoyed, and that was it. There were evenings when it wasn't on at all.

Pat was a watcher only of athletic events and the news, which meant he watched either very late at night—if he was home in time to see the ten o'clock report—or on Saturdays and Sundays. Jill doesn't know where she developed her taste for the soaps, but once she had it, she had it bad. "I scheduled my day around them," she says, which did little for her mind, emotions, or attitude.

The first time Pat left for an extended scouting trip, Jill was devastated. Of course, he'd been on dozens of similar trips before, but this was something new for her. Her father hadn't been much of a business traveler. He was usually home every night at five. Jill didn't expect that with Pat's line of work, but a long trip? She was hurt. He wondered if he would have to face the same reaction every time he left for any length of time.

Pat, who would have been busy during a good year, found himself exhausted during a difficult one. The Bulls were doing well and attendance was up, but he and Dick Motta were feuding, and Pat had no friends in high places anymore. He told Jill none of this.

The Bulls made the 1973 NBA play-offs and faced the mighty Los Angeles Lakers, who were expected to blow them out in four, at most five, games. Incredible effort by the plucky Bulls, however, pushed the Lakers all the way to the seventh game at the Forum in Los Angeles. The Bulls had the favorites on the ropes with a comfortable lead and just two minutes to go. It would have been one of the most dramatic upsets in the history of pro basketball.

Then disaster struck. The fans went crazy as the Lakers scored every time they went down the court, and the Bulls couldn't buy a shot. Were they choking? It didn't appear so yet. They just needed to hang on, hang on, hang on. They still led with just a few seconds left when the Lakers stole the ball and their star guard, Gail Goodrich, scored on an off-balance, twisting, spinning miracle shot to put the Lakers ahead. Now it was the Bulls' ball with plenty of time to score. And they choked. The ball was passed and passed and passed around, no one willing to risk the shot. The final horn sounded. The Bulls hadn't even attempted the winning shot. A horrible, aching loss.

All it served to do was to bring the front-office problems to bear on Pat. The coach dug his heels in; Pat did the same. The owners came down on the coach's side, and Pat could see his professional life coming apart at the seams. "What was I going to do, tell Jill? Not a chance. I wouldn't dream of saying, 'Boy, Jill have I got my hands full. Things aren't going well. I'm into a hassle with the coach, and this ownership is brutal.' I wasn't going to say that. Did I want to? Would I have loved to have been able to tell her and have her full, unconditional support? That's easy to say in retrospect, but then it never entered my mind. I would have had it from her, but I never bothered to find out. I had married her, promised her security, carried the image of the successful exec, and was going to live up to it."

Late in the spring came a meeting with one of the owners, Lester Crown, where Pat was informed that they were thinking about rearranging things, putting the player personnel and negotiating decisions in the hands of the coach. Pat would be more of the business manager, making office and ticket and promotion decisions. He made it clear that he didn't think he could live with that. He was told that they just wanted to let him know it was in the thinking stages. Should he start sending out resumés? He just didn't know.

Pat sought the counsel of some close Christian friends in the

Chicago area, people he'd worked with in the Fellowship of Christian Athletes. But still he kept Jill in the dark. "Yes, I carefully kept it from her and dreaded when it might appear in the paper or on the news. But I felt that was for her own good. Informing her or seeking her advice or support just didn't seem like an option. Simply not part of the scheme of things. It would have been terribly embarrassing, and I didn't want her to worry."

One of the major problems Pat had with this crisis was that it was unique to him after becoming a Christian. He couldn't understand it, didn't know how to deal with it, couldn't explain it. "I had been successful all my professional life, and especially so during the last five years. Nothing but good things. I guess I felt that as a Christian, nothing bad would ever happen to me. This situation wasn't even a failure on my part. It was unfair, an injustice, a huge misunderstanding. But I was going to suffer and be humiliated for it, and that didn't seem to fit with my brand of faith."

In July Pat was told by the Bulls' owners that the plans were now reality. His responsibilities started and ended with the office and promotions. He knew he had to get out. And in a few days, when the decision was announced and was publicized in the press, he heard from the Baltimore Orioles and the Atlanta Hawks.

Both were looking for general managers and told Pat they assumed from what they'd heard that he was not appreciated in Chicago and would probably be eager for a better situation. He was grateful, and the Baltimore job was particularly appealing because of its East Coast location and its being an entrée back into his first love, baseball.

But he felt he had invested the last five years of his life in basketball and that he should stick with what he knew best. He told Jill—and it was such a momentous conversation that she can still remember where she was standing in their Chicago apartment—that he had two opportunities, one in Baltimore and one in Atlanta, and that he felt either looked better than Chicago. "I'm your wife," she said. "I'll go wherever you go."

Inside she was scared. She had enjoyed being close to her

parents, enjoyed having them join her at almost every game. Pat didn't like her driving across Chicago at night and he didn't feel he had the time to come and get her, so she got into the habit of getting a ride to the games with her parents or someone else and then coming home with Pat. Jill became a true fan by going to all of the games. She got to the point where she even knew what colleges all the players had gone to, when they were drafted, the whole story.

But, despite being a little fearful of the move, Jill had lived in the Chicago area most of her life except for her college years, and the grass looked greener on the other side of the fence no matter whether she was looking south or east. Pat visited Atlanta, liked what he saw, was offered an excellent three-year deal, and took it.

Leaving Chicago was a tearful experience, but as soon as their rented moving truck hit the highway, Pat felt a big load leave his shoulders. Jill would miss her parents, but the trip was fun. They sat with the parakeet in between them and sang and laughed much of the way, especially when one of the outside rearview mirrors broke and she had to hold her compact mirror out the window when Pat wanted to change lanes.

They drove all the way to Atlanta on August 12 and went right into the Omni sports complex where the Hawks played their games. Pat immediately went to work, while Jill went out the next day with the owner's wife to start looking for an apartment. She told Pat she found one she thought they'd like, and he said, "Fine, we'll sign the papers and move into it tomorrow."

"Don't you want to see it first?"

"If you like it, I'll like it."

Jill was frustrated, but she directed her irritation at the Hawks. Couldn't they have given him a half-day to help her look, so she didn't have to do this without his seeing the place? Maybe he could have insisted on it, but what was done was done, and they soon settled in.

It was in Atlanta that Jill decided to be a calmer fan. She saw one of the other executive's wives screaming and carrying on and disputing every referee's call, and she realized that many fans knew who these women were. She developed a calmer approach to her spectating—"unless we're in the playoffs; then I scream along with everyone else and nobody pays attention."

Pat and Jill both liked Atlanta, especially the weather, and they sat under the preaching of Dr. Charles Stanley at the First Baptist Church. Pat threw himself into the work and began speaking again. Unfortunately he discovered within the first month that the situation was, if anything, worse than in Chicago. There was a revolving door for marketing and sales people being hired and fired by the Omni management, and Pat got the feeling the owners didn't have confidence in him. "They made me feel like I didn't know how to put one foot in front of the other," he says. "I knew better, but it was a grueling, humbling year. Here I was with my second 'failure' in a row, and I'd just been married over a year."

Jill became pregnant that fall and expected their first child the following May. Pat was happy but started out thinking that he was going to remain detached from the process. Jill told him she'd like him to be in the delivery room with her. He said no. She said, "At least take the natural childbirth classes with me." He agreed, got excited, and said, "You couldn't keep me away." He was in on Jimmy's birth from start to finish and hasn't missed one since.

With the 1974 NBA draft the next day, Pat was too busy to visit Jill in the hospital for more than a few minutes on the way to work each day. She suffered terribly from post partum blues, accentuated by Pat's absence. If it weren't for her mother coming and for Jill busying herself proofreading Pat's first book, his autobiography, she doubts she'd have kept her sanity. She inflicted quite a silent treatment on him for that offense, and after a few days he forced her to tell him what was wrong. She tried to sidestep it with a, "Nothing," but he was persistent and the truth came out.

"You should have visited me more in the hospital."

"I was very busy."

"Too busy to visit your own wife when she's had your child?"

"Okay, I should have spent more time with you."

"You realize you were wrong?"

"If you say I was wrong, then I was wrong."

"That's not good enough."

"Whatever you say."

Pat passed it off as a "new mother" problem. She just didn't understand the magnitude and complexity of his job. Jill was starting to realize that even when she felt she had gotten Pat's attention by giving him the silent treatment and then crabbing about something he had done or hadn't done, his solution was to quickly acknowledge it and promise to do better in order to keep peace. The problem was, she still didn't really have his attention. He wanted to do whatever would provide tranquility for the moment, but wasn't going to change because he saw he was wrong. All he could see was that she was upset, and that made things uncomfortable, so "tell me what you want." Another of his favorite lines, which she grew tired of hearing, was, "Live and let live."

The next time a situation would arise where he had failed before, for instance not opening the car door for her in front of other people, or going off in the corner to talk basketball with someone when she felt he should stay by her, he might do what she expected. But not because he was a changed man or was more sensitive to her. He was doing it because he didn't want another hassle, didn't want Jill to be in a snit, didn't need another two- or three-day silent treament before being able to drag the problem out of her.

What complicated matters was that even though Jill was starting to catch on to Pat's short-term solutions, it didn't bother her. She didn't, for the moment, care *why* he was trying to change or improve. All that mattered was that things were different for a while, and that satisfied her. The reason there was no long-term healing in the relationship, however, was that she was using whatever tricks she could to manipulate him into acting the way she wanted him to, and Pat was putting out fires and patching things up.

Jill knew Pat's life story, of course, but reading the autobiography reminded her of the reason for its title, *The Gingerbread Man*. Before Pat had become a Christian, he had seen himself running here and there and all about, trying to please himself and satisfy deep inner cravings. He thought himself akin to the nursery rhyme character, the Gingerbread Man, who cried, "Run, run, run as fast as you can, you can't catch me, I'm the Gingerbread Man."

She was thrilled for Pat that God, through Christ, had ended Pat's need to live for himself. But her nagging fear was that there was still a lot of Gingerbread to this man. He was still a one-speed guy and it was all-out. He may have changed his ultimate reason for living, but his style was the same. And she was often the victim.

Jimmy's birth was the highlight of their brief stay in Atlanta. When the Philadelphia 76ers called with the general managership open, Pat couldn't move quickly enough. But while he had been looking to escape since the first month, Jill was under the impression that everything was wonderful until the *last* month. "It was like, one day he told me, and the next day we were going." Jill had known something was going on during the summer of 1974 when Pat said he had to take a trip to Philadelphia and told her not to tell anyone who might call. "That went against my grain anyway. I wouldn't lie, and I wasn't about to pretend that I didn't know where he was. Who'd believe that anyway? Well, sure enough, a Philadelphia sportswriter called and asked me point-blank if Pat was talking with the 76ers about the general-manager position. I said, 'His mother lives close by in Delaware, you know.' The writer said, 'Yeah, I know. Thanks.'"

This would be his dream job. He'd been in Atlanta exactly 365 days, his autobiography had been released, he'd had his first son, and he was getting out of the deal with the Hawks. They were just as eager to let him go, and Jill was still flexible. Philadelphia was close to where Pat grew up, so she knew he'd be happy. He would be working with Irv Kosloff, the same owner he'd enjoyed working for his first year out of baseball. And it was clear he really liked Pat and wanted him back.

Pat even promised Jill her own home in the Philadelphia area.

Chapter Eight

Priorities

Pat and Jill and their two-month-old baby boy lived with Pat's mother in Wilmington, Delaware, while looking for a house. The elder Mrs. Williams drove Jill and Jimmy all over the Philadelphia area looking at everything available. "She was patient and tireless," Jill recalls. "Jimmy and I weren't—he was nursing—but we kept looking."

Meanwhile, Pat was jumping into the new situation with gusto. On the one hand, he had little to lose. The 76ers had won twenty-five of eighty-two games and nine of eighty-two games in the two previous years, so there was nowhere to go but up. The problem, of course, was that they had to start winning quickly because the fans were staying away in droves. The Spectrum, where the Sixers played their games, is a beautiful facility with a huge capacity for avid fans, if . . .

Pat set about trying to build an exciting and successful team, while sprucing up the atmosphere and providing other reasons for attending the games. He found it difficult to commute from Wilmington to work every day, yet it wasn't logical to put his wife and baby in a Philadelphia hotel room either. After they had settled on a new house across the river in Moorestown, New Jersey, and began the waiting period for financing, closing, and moving in, Jill and Jimmy moved back to Illinois to stay with her parents for a month.

In some ways that made things easier, but it also gave Jill

time for assessing her young marriage, her new husband, and their future. Conversations from their honeymoon two years before echoed in her mind. She remembered pouting about Pat wanting to walk all the way down the beach to see the scores every night. "This is ridiculous," he had said. "You're really upset about a stinking, little score? Who cares?"

And she had snapped back, "Right, who cares? My point exactly."

"It was so dumb, looking back on it," she says, "but it was a revelation to me. I had found out early that this man was not living for me. He was living for sports. I always thought that the wife was supposed to be number one, and your job maybe number two or three."

She remembered the discussions about going away for the honeymoon. Pat hadn't had a vacation in ten years; he didn't believe in them—figured if you enjoyed your work, you didn't need to get away from it. "He felt he traveled enough in his job, but he just traveled from airport to airport and airport to hotel and hotel to stadium. No sightseeing, no leisure. For me, the honeymoon was a time to solidify the fact that I had changed gears. I was a wife and part of a marriage now. To him it was as if he had taken a break to get married, and then when he got back to Chicago, he would be back in the swing of things."

The memories of the honeymoon, finally coming clearer than ever before, reminded Jill that the tone of their relationship had been set almost from the beginning. She had wanted room-service breakfast. To her that was the ultimate. She suggested it. Pat pooh-poohed it. He was a man of action, a go-getter. "Let's get up and get going and get our own."

Jill pouted and persisted, maintaining that if it was something that would make her happy, he should order it. He said she should order it if that's what she wanted. She said what she wanted was for him to do it. "And I shouldn't even have to suggest it or ask, and certainly I shouldn't have to tell you."

Finally, the last day of the honeymoon week, he ordered room service. But by then its appeal was erased. He was doing it because she had pestered him about it. Being married had made her bolder in saying what she felt. There was no longer the fear that she would lose him. But he had such unusual faults, little pockets of naiveté about how to treat a woman! Her only recourse, she had thought, was to educate him.

During the brief respite she got in 1974 before moving into her new home, she told her parents none of the problems she and Pat were experiencing. Having the chance to see that Pat's failure to spend enough time with her in the hospital was part of a pattern that began on the honeymoon was not of comfort to her. She was not seeing that there were reasons for Pat's behavior, or that his whole life contributed to his performance as a husband. Rather, she was seeing only the pattern and she worried about the future.

Should she talk to him? He wasn't easy to talk to about problems. He was so eager to mend fences that the basic problems weren't dealt with. And no one enjoys criticism. She had attempted to talk to him about sensitive issues before. One was her desire to adopt a Korean orphan someday, something she had always dreamed of.

Pat wouldn't hear of it, didn't even want to discuss it. "Why?" he would say. "It's a silly idea. Why would you want to do that? I'm not sure I could even love a child that wasn't my own. If you want another child, let's have one of our own." End of discussion, until a few months went by and she raised it again. "Forget that, Jill. I don't even want to think about it."

During the absence, Jill convinced herself that things would be better in their new home. She didn't know Jimmy would be a colicky baby and wouldn't sleep through the night once during his first two years of life. Or that when he was three, she'd have another son, Bobby. It is difficult to determine how much the children had to do with the first real signs of discontent, but in all likelihood, they had very little. The patterns had been established, and it would take settling into their first home to bring everything to a head.

In the fall of 1974 they moved in, and life began as a suburban family of three. Pat was involved in the biggest overhaul and rebuilding program he would ever face in his career, and was busy day and night. The Sixers demanded an enormous amount of work and planning and creativity, not only in drafting and trading, but also in promoting and marketing. With the full backing of the owner, Pat was in a position to, as he puts it, "let 'er rip. And it was a thrilling, exciting, and meaningful time in my career."

Jill thought she was happy. She enjoyed Philadelphia's bigness and the opportunities it afforded her. She had not sung or spoken in Atlanta because they had simply not been there long enough to establish the right contacts. In Philly she could see that, down the road a few years, she would be able to exercise some of her public gifts as well. Not right away, but in the not-too-distant future.

The family was active and Jill was not afraid to take Jimmy anywhere anytime. He went to a lot of ball games with her, and when she felt he'd had enough, she got a sitter and went herself. Pat was speaking more and more frequently, eventually reaching several times a week. He was selling the ball club in the best Bill Veeck tradition, and he was also sharing his faith.

He and Jill had devotions together nearly every night, but, she says, "He wasn't really studying. It was good that we were reading and praying together—unless I was in a snit over something; which was fairly frequently—but neither of us were growing. Pat used his testimony or a few favorite jokes and Christian illustrations in every speech. There came a point when I told him, not too kindly, that he could 'take a pass on this one. Stay home and let me give your speech. I know it by heart; I've got it down cold, every joke, your testimony, every line.' "

Pat viewed Jill during this time as his Rock of Gibraltar—the one given in his life. Choice of life's partner, marriage, home, starting a family, that was all out of the way, taken care of. She was beautiful and talented and a natural with the baby. She could cook and clean and was a good hostess. He liked being seen with her, and they had some good times together. Both were humorous with their sarcasm, and enjoyed teasing each other. All in all, Pat thought of Jill as the perfect wife to accompany him to certain functions or to come home to at the end of a tough day. The only negative was that that didn't seem to be enough for her. "All through that early period with the Sixers, I started hearing the warning signals from my wife." She had complaints and demands, such as:

You don't really talk to me.
We never get time alone anymore.
You've stopped dating me, stopped courting me.
You never hold my hand anymore.
We don't share anything.
You don't tell me anything.
We never get away on vacation.

But these were things he just didn't know if he could work into his schedule. There had to be priorities. Where was he going to draw the line? He was trying his best to provide for his family, and he didn't know how to gear down and do less at work. His first reaction was to argue or dispute the charges, but usually he quickly tried to get the fires doused, patch up the hurt feelings, get some flowers or some candy, bring home a gift, take her out. There were more than a few sessions where he'd hold her hand and say:

"Okay, I'm listening. What do you want to talk about?"

"It's not that, Pat. I want you to talk, to tell me things, to tell me about your plans and dreams or just about your day."

"My days are always pretty much the same, you know that. I don't want to bore you with all that."

"I want you to just hold me then."

"All right, but that's not my personality. I have to be doing, going, moving, accomplishing things that mean something."

"Don't I mean something to you?"

"Of course you do, but I don't see any value in just sitting around on the couch holding hands."

"It means a lot to me."

"Okay, so here I am."

Pout. Three days worth of silence, of only a few words when necessary. "Here are your eggs."

"What's wrong?"

"Nothing."

"No, tell me."

"You hurt my feelings."

"When?"

"The other day."

"How?"

"By something you said."

"What?"

"Saying you didn't want to sit holding my hand."

"All right. I shouldn't have said it."

"And you know why?"

"Because it bothered you."

"And you know why it bothered me?"

"If it bothered you, it bothered you and I shouldn't have said it. Isn't that enough? Can't we be done with it?"

"It made me feel like you didn't value me, didn't want to do what was important to me."

"Okay, you're important; let me take you out to dinner Friday night."

Pat recalls: "I could get the hot poker cooled down temporarily and when things were fine on the home front, I could move on out there to the more important things, the meatier issues."

Jill was somewhat satisfied that she was at least getting attention. "I guess it wasn't the kind I really wanted, but it was something. What I really wanted was to be important enough to him that if we got into an argument fifteen minutes before he had to be to work, he would just be late to work. But I wasn't that high on his priority list, and we both knew it. Of course, sometimes I invented things to be upset about at eight forty-five in the morning, so I would have a good reason to be upset with him when he said, 'I gotta go. Let's talk about this later.' I'd think that if he really loved me, he'd have another ten minutes to straighten out the problem."

Jill made Pat pay each time, and the silent treament was the method. "He didn't always have to come through with a gift or a date or something. I just had to see that he was genuinely trying to reconcile. Then I would let him off the hook."

The trouble was, Pat could never be sure just what would set Jill off because, basically, she was an easygoing, soft-spoken person. She took a long, long time to get angry, but when she did, it settled in like a bad rainy season and usually contained thunderheads from days past, all collected into one big storm. If Pat asked too early what was wrong, he got nowhere. There was too much stored up for it to come out that easily. He had to pay first; he'd go crazy with the one- and two-word answers, the huffiness, the little signs that he was in the doghouse. All his pet names for her or his little idiosyncrasies would get a sneer, if they weren't ignored outright. He got tired of trying to pull her up out of the pits of depression and occasionally asked her, "Do you *enjoy* being this way all the time?"

To her own chagrin, Jill says, "I probably did."

Pat just wanted peace. He had an ability to divorce himself from the specific problem at hand and suggest that they discuss it another day, in hope that it would blow away and she'd get over it. That never happened.

If anything, the years up to that point in the Williamses' marriage were as significant as all the years following. For what happened from there on was an escalation of the problems inherent in the type of courtship they had, the patterns of communication established as early as their wedding day and honeymoon week, and the interaction they became used to during those first two years.

In many ways, their problem became repetitive and Pat, for one, got used to it. There were certain prices he had to pay for tranquility at home, and while they were niggling, often frustrating, prices, they were small in comparison to the return. He had what he felt was a good marriage. At least it was the one area of his life he didn't have to worry about.

A recitation of all the fights and confrontations from the second year up to the eighth would serve little purpose and might prove redundant, but it is important to outline some of the major shifts in growth and the mileposts in the escalation of the problems.

In 1975, during a week-long conference at Camp of the
Woods in upstate New York, Pat became convinced that he
should be spending a fixed amount of time every day in serious
Bible reading. He committed himself first to reading, then to
meditating, and then—as he saw the immediate benefits to his
spiritual life—to studying with an open commentary before
him. (Four years later he would add a commitment to memorizing a verse of Scripture a day to his regimen, along with all
his other duties and obligations.)

Bobby was born in 1977—induced in time for the NBA draft
so Pat could "draft" him the way he had Jimmy in 1974. Already the five-bedroom development house was becoming too
small. One of the bedrooms was packed with hundreds upon
hundreds of sports and Christian books, most of which Pat had
read; and—save for the sports books—Jill had read more than
half of them. Another bedroom was a guest room because
Jill's parents and Pat's mother visited quite often, always
shielded from the marital problems smoldering just beneath
the surface.

Credit Jill with never bad-mouthing her husband to her
family. They were, however, aware that things weren't just
right. It wouldn't surprise them terribly when the truth eventually came out.

When Jill snapped back from the birth of Bobby, she was
eager to get out and get involved in ministry again. It had been
too long since she exercised her gifts, and she needed the out-
let. She began singing at functions where Pat spoke, but this
too became a sore spot between them.

Pat would tell her of a speaking engagement he had accepted. She would ask if he had mentioned that she could
come and sing. He had not. But he would call the organizer.
"Fine, it's all right. You can sing." But when she arrived, she
would discover that she was either overdressed or under-
dressed.

"Why didn't you tell me this was formal?"

"I didn't know."

"Why didn't you ask?

"I didn't think it was important."

"Well, it is! It's terribly embarassing to be here in a short dress when everyone's wearing long."

"What's the difference? You're the singer. You shouldn't look like everyone else."

"Next time I would like to know in advance."

And Pat would turn over a new leaf. That became a new wrinkle, but a regular one. Pat was *always* turning over a new leaf. And he meant it every time. And she believed him every time. "Like the dog who gets kicked every time he answers the master's call, yet keeps coming back for more, I just hoped and prayed and believed Pat really had changed each time. But he never had."

That was unusual for Pat, because he was the type who when he set his mind to something would do it obsessively. In 1978 when the running craze really hit and the natural-food literature abounded, he turned over new leaves in both areas. He had always been a jogger, but now he would run and run hard, six miles a day. He got to the point where he was running an hour and twenty minutes a day or more.

And the health food! When he swore off refined sugar and preservatives and salt, he went to whole grains and natural foods in a big way. There was no turning back. Jill made the same commitment, but she wasn't above splurging now and then, which—of course—became another area of argument. Pat could become parental with his take-charge attitude and his seniority in age. While he was suggesting what she should or should not watch on TV or listen to on the radio, he might also give her a verbal "pop" if she wanted to order dessert. For the most part she suffered in silence.

When Jill became pregnant with Karyn, she knew she had to find more house. Again, that was all right with Pat if she wanted to do the looking. She had been searching for a year or so, but she got serious about it now. She finally located a huge, old colonial on a tree-lined lot, also in Moorestown. It had bedrooms and bathrooms galore and enough nooks and crannies and extra rooms and potential for her creative juices that she fell in love with it. That house and the work it would require, along with the prospect of a third child, gave Jill plenty to look forward to.

Pat was pleased to be able to buy her the "new" old place and was excited about another child too. That would be okay, all right, fine. He would want to be in on the delivery, as always. And he would plan to visit Jill more than once or twice in the hospital, even though he was busier than ever. He'd learned that lesson the hard way. But the visits would be just to keep the peace, not because he knew she particularly needed him right then. (Ironically, because of a power failure, Jill delivered by the light from an auxiliary power source and returned home with baby Karyn just nine-hours old. Pat didn't even get the chance to visit.)

With his running and memorizing and reading and meditating and studying and watching what he ate, Pat had added about as much to his schedule as a full-time executive and almost full-time speaker can. The demands of the job were still enormous, and he admits he was working "to a large degree, out of fear. I think in pro sports, most of us do. It's that fear of failure. You're so visible, so naked. Your mistakes are magnified. You foul up a draft or butcher a trade, whatever you do, it's right out there for the media and public and your owners and your colleagues to see and dissect. You work almost out of desperation, but you love the challenge. Love it or not, there's no let up, no time for you to drop your guard or lose your concentration."

Pat was fully committed then to the physical, spiritual, and professional aspects of his life. And he thought things were fine at home. Jill's "sessions" were something he had come to expect. He didn't like them; he got tired of them. They seemed to be coming less frequently now anyway, and if they were the biggest problem he would face outside the office, he could live with that. As long as he had ways to get her out of sulking, pouting, crying, or silence, he was happy.

Jill wasn't.

Chapter Nine

Communication

Jill saw Pat throwing himself into new pursuits, but nothing she could point to and say, "See, my husband is ruining our marriage with this bad habit." With her third baby in five years, she was exhausted, trying to run the house and manipulate Pat enough to get some of his attention some of the time. It was all she could hope for.

Their devotions together became less frequent. He was busier; she was retiring earlier. They hardly spoke in the morning. How she would have longed for a little freshly squeezed orange juice in bed before starting a grueling day! Just once, as a surprise. But that would have been too much to hope for.

Pat was up and running before dawn, and by the time he got back and showered and shaved and dressed for work, he was ready for a quick bite as the kids finished their breakfasts. Then he'd peck Jill on the cheek, deflect any imagined or real issues she wanted to bring up at the last minute, and cart Jimmy off to school while she drove Bobby to preschool.

The card with his daily memory verse, which he had carried while jogging so he could read it as the sun came up, was tucked in with his other most recent ones in the visor of the car, and he studied them as he drove to work.

Sometime during the day, as was his custom no matter where he was or what he was doing, he would call Jill at home. Checking in. Telling her he loved her. Never missed. Even on road trips, even in California. But she was less and less fun to talk to on the phone. Many days he wished he hadn't called. But it was a ritual, something that Jill was grateful for deep down, but a ritual nevertheless.

"I love you, Jill."

Silence.

"I love you," he'd repeat.

"Uh-huh."

"I love you."

"Right."

"I love you."

"Thanks, Pat."

"I love you."

Resignedly, she'd mutter, "I love you, too."

He thought it was a game. She was sincerely having trouble saying it.

Jill was eager to get back in shape after her pregnancy because she knew she needed to get out, to start singing again, to do something, anything, for herself. Even then, she feared, she would be asked to sing only because she was Pat's wife, and not for herself. It wasn't that she wasn't ministry conscious, but did everything she did have to be associated with Pat? Could she not be known for something on her own?

She had always been diametrically opposed to any feminist agenda, yet without realizing it, she was facing some similar struggles. She was living in the shadow of a man. She was, for now at least, pretty much limited to her house. She was working, serving, exhausting herself for others. She was anonymous. And here was her well-known and respected husband out telling people how they could be victorious. "Get into your Bible, get into memorization, come to Christ, live for God." Pat was Joe Christian. And she was Mrs. Joe Christian. Only she felt the opposite, and she knew Pat too well to appreciate his success and popularity as a speaker.

Whom could she go to? Whom could she tell? And what would she say? My husband is too good. He's always reading and studying his Bible and memorizing Scripture. He runs to keep in shape. He's devoted to his job as one of the busiest people for one of the most successful basketball franchises in America. He speaks every chance he gets, sharing his faith and encouraging people in a deeper walk. And since he's been serious about his Bible study, he has a varied speaking approach, always something fresh. Even his humor is expanding. What was he doing wrong? She knew, but she couldn't say.

She'd long since given up suggesting that they adopt Oriental children. That was apparently a closed subject. She felt she would soon be getting too old to have more of her own, yet she had enough love and room for others. Hadn't she fantasized about running an orphanage since she was a child?

It helped some for her to figure out over the years that Pat was basically a broad-brush guy, while she was into details. That was why he couldn't see the importance of making sure she had enough information to be able to dress appropriately for each singing engagement. He didn't think those details were important, because to him they were not. It amazed her, though. In his work, he was specifics crazy. Everything was worked out in minute detail. He made sure of it. But she never benefited from any of that.

Neither did she get any of his creativity. In promotions and marketing he was known as the new Bill Veeck. Pat Williams was creativity personified. Yet he never surprised her. "You're so predictable," she would charge. "You haven't surprised me for years. There's no spontaneity in our life. Plan something. Do something for me like you do for the Sixers."

Pat had heard that a lot. "When you come home, the creativity ends. It's boring." That hurt. No one likes to be criticized, but Pat was creatively exhausted. He was pouring everything into the Sixers and into his speaking ministry, and the very thought of having to crank up his creativity at home too made him weary.

"I was spent," Pat recalls, "but Jill kept saying she was getting the crumbs, the leftovers. She knew that because I was healthier and studying and reading and memorizing more that there were even more resources for me to draw from, and still she was getting nothing, while thousands of Sixers fans and my speaking audiences were getting it all."

As Jill got herself back in shape, regained her strength, and started circulating more, she felt better. She felt a little guilty about getting a sitter so often, but she needed to get out, to get away. One thing that helped her maintain her sanity during the first few months after Karyn was born was that she was not being too analytical.

"In fact," she says, "if you had asked me at that time if I was happy or had a good marriage, I would probably have said yes, in spite of everything. Many of my friends tended to be in the same boat, only they had different problems. Maybe their husbands surprised them now and then with a rose or a telegram or something special. But then their husbands were always out playing golf on Saturday and mine wasn't. So I figured it was even."

Jill had never been a psychology buff. She found that if she didn't have anyone to talk to about a problem, rather than analyze every feeling, she would pretend it didn't exist or that she was resigned to it. She was fooling herself. But not for long.

When Pat was around she was more aware of her frustration. She was forever making lists and confronting him. "Here are three things: one, flowers; two, dinners out; three, do some of my things. If you could just do that for me once in a while. Now I've been honest, you be honest with me. Tell me. I can take it. What would you like me to do for you or change or whatever? Anything. What?"

And he would say, "Jill, I wouldn't change a thing about you. I think we have a perfect marriage."

That wasn't what she wanted to hear. She would have been glad to give, to compromise, to do her part. Anything to get him off square one. The next time they discussed it, she would rattle off dozens of complaints, suggestions, areas that needed improvement. "Now, Pat, you must have one thing you don't like about me, something you think I should change."

"Well, you know I don't like when you get depressed and sulk and refuse to tell me what's wrong. But other than that, no, nothing. Everything's fine." And he believed that with all his heart.

In private he told her she was the best cook ever. "Why don't you ever tell anyone else that?"

"Okay, next time I will."

"You never kiss me in front of people."

"Okay, if that's what you want." And when she would come to a Sixers game, he would greet her with a peck on the forehead. It wasn't that she wanted to be wrestled to the floor. She just wanted to be acknowledged as the man's wife, not assumed to be his cousin.

And every time, he promised to turn over a new leaf. "Right, Pat. I have a yard full of new leaves. And they've all turned old and yellow. They've all decayed." The point had come where, although she didn't believe he would change, she *wanted* to believe he would. "But I sort of knew better."

Getting him to do what *she* wanted to do was a major project. "Can't we do something together? Anything!"

"Okay, I was going to go to the Phillies game tomorrow. Wanna go?"

"Why does it always have to be something you want to do. Let's go to *The Nutcracker Suite.*"

"*The Nutcracker Suite?* Oh, Jill! I can't think of anything I'd less rather do."

"See? We always do what you want to do whether I want to or not, but when it's something *I'd* enjoy, then it's another story."

"Okay, all right, we'll go to *The Nutcracker.*"

"Really?"

"Sure."

"You really want to?"

"Sure."

"Are you sure?"

"If it'll make you happy."

They went. Pat was bored to tears, but he endured. "Now," he said, "I went. You owe me one. How about the Phillies?"

"Let's talk percentages," Jill would counter. "What percentage is one or two concerts out of four hundred and ninety-five ball games?"

When she bugged him enough about going somewhere, he'd often say, "Why don't you go? Go with some of your friends. I won't mind. I have to watch the NCAA finals on television, but there's no reason why you can't go."

When her friends expressed sympathy that she had to go with them instead of with Pat, she covered for him. "I really enjoy it," she'd say. "He's tied up, but at least I get to go. He's good to let me go by myself." But he hadn't been so good on purpose, she says. "He was getting rid of me so he could watch the tournament in peace."

So, Jill was losing her "no freedom" argument. In fact, she had too much freedom.

By now, of course, she felt she had gotten to know Pat fairly well. Later she would realize she hardly knew him at all, but back then she resented not benefiting from the qualities she was aware of. "He was emotional and sensitive enough to hate telling a ballplayer he'd been traded. On the other hand, I always felt he was extremely conceited. We talked about it more than once, and it was a sore point with him. Although he was shy, I thought he appeared cocky and I was sure people perceived him that way. I didn't want anyone to think badly of my husband, so I told him what I thought. I probably went about it the wrong way because he just laughed it off and said he didn't think people thought that about him."

There were other things about Pat that Jill was dissatisfied with. She wished he was as careful about certain things as he had been when they were dating. Things like washing his car, shining his shoes, having his hair cut by someone who knew what he was doing. She asked several times if he didn't want to look into the possibility of contact lenses. "It wasn't that I had anything against men in glasses, but some look better without them, and I thought Pat was much handsomer without. He wouldn't even discuss it."

As a Chicago-based bachelor, Pat had a vice. Clothes. With a good salary and only himself to spend it on, he was always dressed in the latest fashions. Now in Philadelphia, secure at the top of his profession, plain suits were fine with him. Jill thought he would look good with some casual clothes occasionally. Maybe some boots or jeans or a pullover sweater.

She also thought he'd lost his healthy, athletic look, ironically, because of his severe health-food diet and his jogging. He was running so far and so hard and so regularly that he lost fifty pounds and began to look gaunt. He'd lost upper-body tone and strength. His face was skeletal and his shoulders were thin. His suits hung on him. She even bought him a set of weights. With his cheap haircut, graying hair, glasses, and thinness, to Jill he had aged twenty years in ten.

Early in the spring of 1981 Jill had to call and cancel a singing engagement because she had flu symptoms that morning. With the burden of the difficult phone call off her back, she hoped she'd be able to relax and start recuperating. Yet even lying down didn't help.

She didn't feel horribly sick, but she thought maybe a quick doctor's visit would be the solution. Dr. Joseph Winston was a Christian and an acquaintance of the family. She phoned. No, they couldn't see her until the next day. Suddenly she was in tears, something inside telling her that she shouldn't wait. "I really have to see him today," she pleaded.

After examining her and sending a blood sample down the hall to the lab, he interviewed her cautiously. "How've you been? How's Pat? Busy?" At the end of the exam he received the lab results and studied them carefully.

"Two things," he said. "Number one, it's my guess your husband isn't spending enough time with you. Am I right?"

Jill shrugged, fighting tears.

"If he spends time, you're not getting enough attention?"

She didn't answer.

"You have a blood disease, and it's quite serious. I don't want you to drive home. I'll take you and you can arrange to get your car later. I'm prescribing antibiotics and complete bed rest for several days. And I want to see you in two weeks or hear from you anytime during that period if you feel it necessary."

Pat called his mother to help out around the house and

checked in on Jill occasionally. "I need to tell you what else the doctor told me," she said. "He wondered if you were spending enough time with me."

"What?"

"That's right. That's what he said."

Pat shook his head. "How in the world would he know how much time we spend together? We live in the same house! Besides, it's none of his business."

"All I know is that that's what he said, and if people who hardly know us wonder that, don't you you think maybe you should start thinking about it?"

He ignored the question. "What did you tell him?"

"What *could* I tell him? I didn't tell him anything."

In two weeks the doctor told Jill that the disease was much more serious than he had even let on. "You would not have made it if you'd tried to wait until the next day for treatment," he said. "It's a quick and deadly killer." She suffered its effects for months, even into the 1981-1982 pro-basketball season when she was constantly battling colds and fever and sore throats.

Pat hadn't seen the doctor's comment as a significant issue. Jill didn't bring it up again, but she was on his case about everything else. At times he felt he knew what she wanted, and he was reluctant to commit to it. His fear was that she wanted his core, his being, his mind, his soul. She wanted to know what was in there. What was going on. "But what if I had let her in?" he recalls wondering. "What if I completely opened up and was then rejected or scorned. Then it would be all over. There would be nothing left. I couldn't risk that. And I don't know many men who could."

"All we talk about is the weather and kids," Jill would tell him. She wanted intimate bonding, the sharing of career and family goals, aspirations, objectives, interests, hobbies, and time. Pat agrees now that they were critical areas to her, and he doesn't argue with their importance. But getting to them and getting them done was another story.

"We don't have *any* common interests," she charged. "No common time spent doing *anything*. Nothing as a family."

Pat heard that so many times he wanted to scream. "I knew she was right, but how do you do it? You feel like you're fighting a swarm of bees. I couldn't fend them off. I was busy running, reading, studying, memorizing, running the kids to school, working all day, traveling, scouting, going to pro and college games. I was the type who had to have every phone call returned, every piece of paper off my desk, the lights turned out, and the door locked."

Most nights he arrived home to an upset wife. "But I didn't see any hope for changing anything. I was a perfectionist and that's just the way it was. Evangelical Bible teacher and preacher Lehman Strauss once told me he was convinced—from his many years of counseling—that most men have their identities wrapped up in what they do for a living and how well they do it. My whole life I'd had the philosophy that there wasn't anything I wouldn't do to get the job done. That was the reason I had gotten to the place I had. But it took its toll."

Years before, Jill had confided in their mutual friend, author Marabel Morgan, that she wished Pat would just sit and talk with her sometimes. "Pat," Marabel said, "promise me you'll give her ten uninterrupted minutes a day."

"Yeah, sure, Marabel, okay. I can do that."

"Just ten minutes for her alone."

"Right. I'll do it."

He tried. Several times. Jill held that broken promise over his head for years.

During that whole time, people often told Jill, "It must be wonderful being married to him."

"Oh, yes," she would say, without a trace of sarcasm. "It's exciting meeting famous people and getting to go to fun places." *If they only knew,* she thought.

Some did know. Her parents for two. But anytime they suggested anything negative or asked probing questions, Jill was quick to defend Pat. She knew his schedule and his priorities as well as he did. But her excuses for him weren't necessarily calculated. She was a different person in front of family and guests, yes, but she believed her excuses too. "I was beginning to pretty well have myself snowed."

During the fall of 1981, Jill first started wondering if maybe this was the way life was supposed to be. She didn't want to give in to that thinking just yet, but somewhere in the recesses of her mind she feared that she would only make herself more unhappy if she kept wanting and hoping for the kind of marriage and family life that simply wasn't going to happen.

By winter in late 1981, Pat and Jill became fairly distant from each other. "I just had trouble being informal with him," she says. "I was keeping him at a distance, probably hoping to minimize my hurt feelings."

Outside she felt she was doing pretty well, fooling all her friends. Even the ones who knew her well were still in awe of Pat and would not have been able to believe or understand the kind of problems she was having with him. She couldn't fool the kids, though. One day five-year-old Bobby asked her, "Why aren't you happy, Mommy?"

One of the things that made her particularly unhappy was having to sit alone or with friends, and not Pat, at the Sixers games. She wouldn't see him from the time she arrived until halftime when he might greet her with a handshake or, at best, a peck on the forehead. Occasionally he would muss her hair the way he might that of a little boy, which didn't thrill her either.

There were times when she would go to the game by herself and sit craning her neck to see into the press box during the first quarter, trying to get Pat's attention for even a wave. But if it wasn't forthcoming, she couldn't fake one, because then people might look up and see that Pat wasn't even looking at her. She often grew tired of waiting and just watched the game, waiting until halftime for her audience with the G.M. When she'd hassle him later for not showing her more attention, he'd remind her that other general managers sit in the press box with the scouts and guests and press, and obviously, "I couldn't kiss you in front of everybody anyway."

The day was coming when he'd wish he had.

Chapter Ten

Short-Term Solutions

Pat's parental nature really began getting to Jill. He would come home from a college game or some other function, walk right in front of her while she was watching her favorite TV program, and switch the set off.

"You have no right to do that!"

"Well, you say we never talk. Don't you want to talk to me?"

"Oh, sure! You don't talk to me for weeks, and now when I'm right at the best part, you walk in and turn it off without even asking. You treat me like you're my father!"

Their arguments grew worse and more frequent, with Jill winding up screaming at Pat. "It was the only way I could get a reaction from him. He wouldn't look at me, would turn on the radio, would look off in the distance, anything to keep from having to respond. I'd beg and whine and cry, and rather than trying to calm me down with the right words, he'd just frustrate me more by fathering me or sitting there so passively that I wanted to punch him."

While neither of them ever came close to physically harming the other, they both recall this period with references such as Jill's above. She could have punched him. For his part, he says he can see how a non-Christian might be driven to spouse abuse. He thought he was being a peacemaker, but all he was doing was making Jill angrier. She would have loved to have had him shout back, just once. Even negative attention would be better than no attention.

Jill found herself getting a sitter more often than ever and getting out to record music, shop, and even take flying lessons. Her father had piloted a small plane, and it was something she had always wanted to do. Karyn was in nursery school two mornings a week, so she was free. But when she felt like taking a whole day, she just called someone to pick up Karyn.

After her own album was finished, she found other reasons to hang around the recording studio. She sang backup for other artists and generally became a "studio junkie." If she wasn't singing, she was watching, talking with musicians, whatever. "I was just hoping Pat would notice I was gone. Let him come home to a sitter a few times and see if he wondered where I'd been. He wouldn't even ask."

Sometimes, during the evening, she would tell him, "I want to go out."

"Fine."

She would go to a shopping mall and shop until the place closed, then drive around until very late. No questions. No curiosity. "Beyond sports, he isn't interested in anything," she decided. "Least of all, me."

Did she think he'd lost interest in her? "Not lost. Never had. I asked him, 'Do you really want to know what's inside me? Do you really want to know what I'm thinking, where I'm going, what I'm doing, what I'm buying?' And he'd say, 'Do you want to tell me?' "

The few times they had together were usually in the car on the way to and from a speaking and singing engagement. Jill would begin a conversation, and Pat would interrupt it by turning on the radio to get the latest scores. "The basketball I could understand," she says. "That was his life and our livelihood. Even then, the scores weren't going to change between then and the midnight news. But he had to know now. And not just basketball. Even golf, for Pete's sake. I told him he wouldn't die from not knowing, but still he had to listen. Even if he had just said, 'Give me a second to get the scores and then

I'm yours for half an hour,' that would have been fine. I wouldn't have minded the interruption a bit."

Pat took Jill with him to Los Angeles for the fourth game in the 1982 NBA playoffs between the Sixers and the Lakers. The Sixers lost and trailed in the seven-game series three to one, but Pat wasn't particularly disappointed. The Lakers were clearly the better team that day.

Win or lose, his and Jill's plan was to enjoy a leisurely Mexican dinner after the game. As they wheeled into the Los Angeles traffic jam, a romantic FM station played soft music on the radio. That is, until Pat switched the dial to the Angels-Tigers baseball game. "It was a game that meant nothing to me or to anyone else outside California or Michigan," he admits. "But we had been to their game the night before, and it was sports, so . . ."

The evening was ruined. It was as if he had stabbed Jill in the heart. She let him know, unloading her anger and pain. He tried to make it right, but it was too late.

Jill's mind was on her marriage more and more. She was reading, listening, talking, studying about it. "I should have been thrilled that he was letting me do my own thing, discover myself, become aware of my possibilities. But that isn't really what I wanted. I wanted him. I wanted him to care, to notice. That's all." She would repaint or repaper a room. Or even completely rearrange the furniture. Unless she pointed it out to him, he rarely seemed to notice.

During the summer of 1982, they took trips to Bermuda and China. Even there, Jill felt like excess baggage. It wasn't that the trips weren't exciting and fascinating; she just found that she wasn't having as good a time with Pat as she often had without him. Not only did he not seem to care, he was getting on her nerves. She fought the feeling, but she was falling out of love with him. The very things that had attracted her to him in the first place now turned her off. She resented his idiocyncrasies, his perfectionism, his obsession with sports and statistics, his photographic memory, his gift for gab.

In Bermuda she was quite taken with the mopeds, the motorized bikes that would putt-putt you anywhere you wanted to go. That, along with her interest in flying, were indications that she was hungry to flee. To flee him, her home, her family, her situation. But she didn't know it yet.

While with Pat in China on the NBA tour, Jill was again flooded with her desire to adopt an Oriental child. She had no idea why God had put that on her heart, but she knew He had long before she was married. When the Vietnamese boat people were in the news, she really "had the bug," but Pat had cured her of that. She had learned to put it out of her mind. She surprised herself that she was able to, but Pat had been so adamant that he would never be able to love such a child that she knew it was out of the question.

Out of the question and out of her mind, but not out of her heart. The Chinese children were so endearing! It had been so long since she had raised the issue with Pat that she hardly remembered the conversation—except the result of it. In the hotel lobby, before a tour with the missionary guide, John Bechtel, a friend who had grown up in China, Jill cautiously ventured, "Ask John how difficult it would be to adopt a Chinese baby."

"Jill! C'mon, cut it out. Don't bother him with that."

"Well, you could just ask."

"Forget it, I'm not going to ask him that."

Later, when Jill decided to ask John herself, Pat cut in with an apologetic chuckle. "Yeah, John, she has this crazy idea that she's gonna take one of these kids home with her." John explained why it's almost impossible to adopt a Chinese, and later Pat got an earful about his making fun of her over it.

Back home, Jill was frequently finding reasons to beg off from singing when Pat spoke. That was difficult, because they now had Barbara Albrecht, a friend in Riverside, New Jersey, handling their arrangements. The more sophisticated their dealings, the more difficult it was for Jill to cancel at the last minute.

On the engagements when she did go along to sing, she found herself playacting perfectly. "I *was* that other person," she says. "I was the happily married wife of an impressive speaker and big-time executive." And even on the way home, she would discover that for a time she had been transformed. Fresh from ministering through her music and hearing her husband turn on a crowd with his speaking, and high on the compliments they both received, they'd start home happy. It was as if they really were the couple the people thought they were.

Pat didn't seem to need any strokes, even though she complimented him on the job he'd done. They might discuss how a certain joke or anecdote went over, and then Jill would wait in vain for a comment about her singing. After about forty-five minutes, she was through playacting and was dying now for any response. "So, did I sing all right, or not?"

"Of course you did, Jill. You always sing beautifully. You're my favorite singer. Didn't the people clap for you? Didn't they come up and tell you how much they enjoyed it? They certainly told me they enjoyed you."

"Yes, they told me, but it doesn't mean a thing unless I hear it from you."

Neither remembers when they had their last fight, but it was sometime during the late summer or early fall of 1982. Jill had screamed at him, and he had responded as usual, hardly saying anything. He figured it wouldn't do any good if they were both screaming, and it wasn't in his personality to raise his voice anyway. "He probably hasn't more than twice in our entire marriage," she says.

But during the last hot one, Jill was at her cutting, sarcastic best. "As a singer, I had good breath control and volume," she says. "He'd be sitting there, not saying anything, and I'd be yelling, 'Are you listening to me? Do you really hear what I'm saying to you?' Sometimes he'd look at me, probably wondering, *What have I married?* 'I was not this way when I was younger,' I'd continue. 'You have driven me to be a screaming shrew!' He laughed it off and that got me even madder. 'You don't care enough to even argue with me!' "

"Do you like being this way?" he asked.

"What else can I do? You've made me this way!"

It usually took Jill five sentences, each increasing in volume, to get Pat finally to say, "All right, Jill, I'm sorry. Can we please drop it?" All she wanted was for him to apologize immediately, admit he was wrong, and say that he would try to do better next time. Here they'd been married for years and all she was getting was a resigned apology designed to get a screaming wife off his back.

After that last shouting performance, Jill decided she had had enough. There would be no more screaming. Apparently, Pat was not going to change. She was going to stop making sure that every little misdemeanor was brought before the court. She couldn't beg, plead, pray, badger, holler, or humiliate him into changing, so she was going to accept him the way he was. She wasn't going to like it, but she was going to live with it the way a person lives with a handicap; make the best of it and quit praying for a miracle. The upshot was, she was out of the house more and for longer periods than ever.

Her own devotional life was on the skids. She prayed, but only for herself. She rarely read her Bible, despite Pat's constant potshots about it. Every once in a while he would try to talk to her when she was in a good mood. He would be kind and gentle and fatherly and he would chat amiably about her need to be quiet and submissive.

"Yeah," she responded. "The minute I lie down and be quiet and submit, you're going to walk all over me. No way I'm going to let that happen."

"You don't know that I would do that, Jill."

"Wanna bet? I've got a degree in it."

She had turned into something she despised. "Joe Christian going out to speak again tonight?" she asked. "What're you going to tell 'em tonight, Pat? How to be the perfect Christian husband?"

"I got really good at that," she recalls. "And I hated myself."

Jill went to the Sixers 1982 home opener that fall, and then began finding reasons not to attend the rest of the games. She was too tired, or under the weather, or simply didn't want to.

She had her own things going, and she was frankly more at ease by herself or with friends than with Pat. Sometimes she planned to go but then somehow didn't make it. Pat told her people were asking about her.

"I just didn't feel like going," she'd say.

"All right. Whatever you want." She had always been very interested in the team. But now it seemed she couldn't care less. When she missed a game against the arch-rival Boston Celtics in November, Pat knew something was wrong. He didn't want to force her. He only wanted her to come if she wanted to. But it hurt him and bothered him that she didn't. She would have liked to hear that. But she didn't. And by now she was too tired, mentally and physically, to fight. She had given up hope and was simply doing her own thing.

One night Jill rode with friends to a Fellowship of Christian Athletes rally where she was to sing and Pat was to emcee. He drove straight from the office. When it was over, Jill came to him.

"Would it be all right if I rode home with my friends?"

"What are you talking about?"

"I just want to ride home with them, that's all. What's the difference? I rode here with them."

"And how is that supposed to look? Forget it. No way."

Pat had put his foot down, feeling what he considered righteous indignation. But when she rode home with him, in his mind the crisis was over. He had not seen the incident as the symptom it was.

Confrontations were becoming less frequent. When Jill got in at two in the morning, Pat might ask where she'd been. "Just forget it," she'd say.

"What do you mean forget it? You come in well after midnight and I'm supposed to forget it?"

"It doesn't matter if I come home or not anyway, so what's the difference?"

"Of course it matters. You know that. You know I care about you, so how can you say it doesn't matter?"

"Just forget it."

"Jill, don't do that. It's just not right. It's not you." And it wasn't. She was a conservative homebody, family oriented. Now she was playing, out with friends until all hours.

Jill recalls that Pat was probably so tired of trying to pull her up out of the pits of depression by now that he had no other solutions. If she didn't want to discuss it, he'd let it drop. Flying lessons, singing, hanging around the studio, shopping, out driving by herself, all these got her out of the house and kept her out for hours at a time. He knew something wasn't right, but at least she had quit all the screaming and nagging. Maybe she was maturing. He just hoped she'd grow out of the busyness that took her away from the kids.

During this time Jill began dressing a lot flashier. "She looked fantastic, of course," Pat says. "She had the figure for it, but still it wasn't right. I didn't know it at the time, but now I see that she was seeking emotional intimacy outside the home. If the only place she could find that was with others, then that was where she would go. That was where people listened to her, looked at her when she spoke, seemed to care for her. They saw her worth and treated her that way. There was nothing illicit going on, but she was getting emotional strokes there that she so desperately wanted from me."

Pat hadn't changed either. If he had time for the kids, it was only between ball games on cable television. When they first got cable, Jill thought it would at least keep Pat at home more. Games he used to have to travel to he could now scout at home. But dozens of games were available around the clock, games he wouldn't have been able to travel to anyway. Now, besides getting up early and coming home in the early evening, he was also up half the night watching basketball on television. He couldn't think of a better setup. Besides being Pat's vocation, basketball became an addiction via cable TV.

"My wife was in what I considered an irrational period, going through something apparently, but she was a little more carefree and happy-go-lucky, so that was all right. My home was rock solid. I had cute, healthy, seemingly well-adjusted kids, kids I would romp with for ten minutes or a half-hour between important responsibilities. I had a wife who looked as good if not better than when we married, was a consummate cook, a great housekeeper and mother, a singer who still occasionally sang when I spoke. I had it made. My home was my refuge and Jill was my rock."

Meanwhile, Jill was just resigned to her role and her inattentive husband. If this was the way it was going to be, then this was the way it was going to be and she was going to have some fun along the way. After all, there were advantages to being married to someone like Pat. She had met presidents, superstar entertainers, athletes, you name it. Many friends were envious of her jet-setting life.

It was common for her to tell Pat she felt she needed a weekend away. "Sure, go ahead. Get a sitter. That'll be all right." She had quit even asking if he would go with her. She took books and tapes and sheet music and money, and she checked herself into a hotel in a town near an antique village. She read several books, learned some new songs, and went antiquing until she thought she'd seen them all. It was refreshing for her, in a way, but in another it deepened her depression.

She knew that Pat didn't know where she was, probably didn't think or wonder about her, and wouldn't ask when she got back. No questions. Not where were you or what did you do or did you enjoy it. Just nothing. "For all he knew, I could have been having an affair. It's probably a little weird that a woman in my position in the 1980s *wasn't*, and I suppose there were people who thought I was. I was never attracted to anyone else or even tempted, but I did wonder if he'd care if I did." Once she even told him that she should go out and have an affair, "just to get your attention." She knew she was talking irrationally, but her whole being was crying out for him to show some interest in her.

For his part, Pat thought he was being of help. "I figured it was good that she was able to get totally away from it all. I thought it might be the pressures of the bigger house and family that were causing her troubles, so I was happy to arrange the escape."

Strangely, the Williamses own physical relationship had not yet suffered from the disharmony. Perhaps it was because Pat was mostly oblivious to the problems that so deeply affected his wife. Jill had conned herself into thinking that since things could be worse, she should be happy and make the best of it. Her husband wasn't a carouser or a drug addict or a drunk.

But he was a part-time husband. He lived and slept and ate with her and had all the privileges of a married man, while leading the life of a bachelor. His job and his ministry and his body were his top priorities, and Jill and the house and kids, as he said himself, were his refuge. Not a bad deal if you can get it. But he was shortchanging himself too, and he didn't know it.

Jill felt depressed, particularly every morning, dreading another day. Her spiritual life was all but shot. She was able to pray with the kids or at a meal, but she knew the prayers were bouncing off the ceiling. When Pat would challenge her or encourage her in her Bible study and devotional life, she'd say, "What's it to you? Don't start sermonizing. I'm not mad at God, but who else can I blame? You're not changing, and that's what I've been praying for for so long."

In truth, she was afraid to be angry with God. True praying was sporadic. "I don't want You to get mad at me, God, but it doesn't seem like You care about me. If You cared, wouldn't You want me to be happy in my marriage?"

During this period, Pat was reading the final galley proofs of his new work, *The Power Within You,* a motivational book that used the paradoxes of Scripture as its thesis (To be rich, give your money away; to be powerful, humble yourself; to be a leader, be a servant). In it, Pat was sketchy on the marital relationship, but in many ways, honest. He admitted that he was weak in the areas of spending time with the kids and giving his wife the personal time and attention she craved. Yet acknowledging it for the readers didn't change things at home.

Jill's deepest depression hit quickly. It had been building for months, even years, but that late fall of 1982 was the worst time. She acknowledged that Pat, maybe because of the book, was trying a little harder than ever, but he was still patching and taping, not really fixing and changing.

Jill was still going to bed alone and getting up alone. She cried a lot, seemingly for no reason. She took naps that did little good. She was weary, exhausted, listless all the time. She knew something was wrong, but she didn't know what was happening to her, and she was embarrassed to go to anyone for help. Who would believe, with a life and a husband like hers, that anything could be wrong?

But at playacting—living a lie, she calls it now—she was a pro. So good, she even fooled Pat. People would call and ask how she was. "Just fine, great, how are you?" And when there was company, friends, relatives, guests, she pulled the wool over every eye.

Friday night, the 17th of December, 1982, the Williamses hosted a houseful of singers from Word of Life who were in town for a concert. Jill was at her best. The happy homemaker, the perfect hostess. "It was a riotous, great night," Pat recalls. "A marvelous evening."

However, Jill cried herself to sleep that night, as she had so many times before. She was past mad. She was resigned. "I wanted attention from him and I wasn't getting it. If the husband is the head of the wife, why should I have to manipulate him? Regardless of what else I had in my marriage to Pat Williams, I didn't have *him*. And to me that was worse than if I had nothing."

Pat's mother had been involved in a serious automobile accident several weeks before and was now out of the hospital and registered in a rehabilitation facility outside Wilmington, Delaware. On Saturday Pat took the kids to see her. Top priority for that day was to get home in time to watch basketball on TV, first Houston against Syracuse, then the Sixers and the Bullets.

Little did he know that the next day was D Day in his marriage.

Chapter Eleven

Crisis

From a "marvelous evening" Friday with the Word of Life group to a nice, reassuring visit with his mother on Saturday, and then an exciting evening of basketball, Pat waded into a Sunday he would never forget. December 19 will always be an anniversary in the Williams household. It does not carry pleasant memories; however, it was the beginning of the end of a bad marriage and the start of a good one.

It sure didn't seem like it at the time though. The confrontation Pat and Jill had gone through in their living room that day had made the Sixers' party meaningless for Pat. And as he lay there that night, staring at the ceiling he had no idea what he was going to do or how he was going to do it. And if he discovered something, he had no guarantee it would work. Overnight, it seemed to him, he could be losing his wife and family. Jill had never, ever meant as much to him as she did right then.

He could hardly think about what she'd said to him that fateful afternoon without breaking down and crying. Worse yet, he had to be up bright and early the next morning for work. The work went on without a break for his domestic problems. He still felt compelled to run and read and study and memorize and pray. He would not give that up. But now he was like a scared rabbit.

In the morning Pat felt miserable. For the first time in years, he had slept only a few hours. And Jill was padding around the

112

kitchen like a zombie, seemingly unable to talk or smile. To Pat it seemed as though he was trying to communicate with a dead person. She wouldn't look at him, wouldn't respond to him, wouldn't answer him. He pecked her on the cheek as he left and said that he would do whatever was necessary to "work this out." She didn't even nod.

"It was as if she was unfocused," he recalls. "She was confused; she didn't care. I had never seen this side before. This was totally new. The short-term funks I'd witnessed had been calculated and motivated by anger. This seemed more as though she'd been run over by a truck."

Pat called her from the office as usual, but he got one-syllable responses until he finally gave up. He worked hard at keeping his concentration on the job, but tears welled up at odd times. "I was panic-stricken. My confidence was shot. I wasn't in control. My reaction was, have I done this in ten years of marriage? I've somehow caused this! I've done this to the woman I love, and yet I'm not sure what I've done." Pat had once heard Bob Palmer of the Sandy Cove Bible Confer ence say, "A woman can hang in through adversity for a long time, but when she comes to the end of her rope, she dies just as suddenly." He never thought he would see that happen before his eyes in his own home—to his own wife.

Any hope Pat had that things would be different that Monday night were crushed when he got home from work and found Jill slouched in front of the televison, the house a mess, the kids on a rampage, and nothing on the stove for dinner. She hardly acknowledged his presence. She had told him she could promise him nothing, no guarantees about her emotional response. He was discovering what she meant.

A shake of the head or a shrug was the best he could get from her, and it made him break down again. He wanted to beg her to come back, to be the old Jill, to put things back the way they'd been, or at least the way he thought they'd been.

He rustled up something for the kids to eat and tried to wait on Jill, but she wasn't hungry, didn't want or need anything, and went to bed soon after the children did. Pat felt he was on the brink of losing his mind, not because the trauma or the lack of sleep had necessarily caught up with him yet, but simply out of frustration. He would have done or given anything to put his marriage and family life back together, but how could he convince Jill of that when she wouldn't even look at him?

Her face was eerily expressionless, her eyes dark and cold and small. At her best, Jill's eyes flashed brilliantly and her face glowed not only with beauty but with character and life. She was dead, Pat decided. Emotionally dead. *And I killed her.*

He paced the quiet, dim-lit house in frustration for several hours, praying, hoping, wondering, trying to get a handle on the whole situation. He had to admit he had a real fear of what the public reaction might be if his marriage got worse. There had to be an answer, a solution, He couldn't lose everything that mattered to him just like that, could he? He didn't know.

Pat had been reading Chuck Swindoll's new book, *Strengthening Your Grip,* and a quote from it was haunting him: "For God to do an impossible work, He must take an impossible man and crush him."

It was near midnight when he finally poured out his heart to God in total honesty. In a torrent of tears, he cried out, "Lord, do to me whatever you have to. I've got a crisis here that obviously I have caused. Crush me. Show me. Tell me. Help me. What do I do? Remind me what I've done so I can set about changing it. And give me the wisdom and the strength and the power to do it through You."

The answer came quickly, almost too quickly, almost so quickly that Pat might have wished he hadn't asked. God shattered him, broke his heart and his will. He was overwhelmed, washed away with the tears of trauma and guilt and remorse. For the first time in years he saw himself for what he was. He was somehow able to remember all those things that Jill had harped on for a decade. He whipped a pen from his pocket and filled several legal-sized yellow sheets.

Through his tears he scribbled as quickly as he could to keep up with all the areas the Lord was impressing upon him. The statements he wrote down rang true. He was nodding as he wrote, echoing the charges Jill had leveled against him so frequently for so long. Why hadn't he heard? Why hadn't they registered? Why had all his solutions in the past been temporary? Why had his resolve to turn over a new leaf always failed along the way?

Pat knew God was working a miracle in his life as he wrote over sixty items that had troubled Jill and that he had neglected to permanently rectify. It was a heart-wrenching, cleansing experience as he confessed each shortcoming to God and asked His forgiveness. The result he was left with was unlike the short-term vows he'd made in the past. He had been awakened to the misplaced priorities in his life; he knew that he'd been on a success trip, while his priorities, even the good ones like Bible study and jogging and speaking, were all self-motivated and self-gratifying.

In themselves, there was nothing wrong with them. But when they were placed ahead of the relationship that God had joined together, Pat realized, he himself had been the man who was tearing that relationship asunder. His pages were filled with areas God sharply convicted him about, simple everyday things. Things like spending time with Jill in uninterrupted conversation, touching her, holding her, holding her hand, dating her once a week, sitting with her at ball games, taking out the trash, not overstimulating the kids just before bedtime, saying nice things about her in front of people, treating her like a friend, checking into contact lenses, being neater, dressing more fashionably, not being so thin, not spending so much time running, going to bed with her and getting up with her, not reading the paper at the breakfast table, not parenting her, listening to her rather than the radio, looking at her, caring, asking, being creative with her—not so predictable—doing things with her that she liked to do, getting away with her even during the season, being open to adopting an Oriental child, maintaining eye contact with her, sending her flowers, sending cards to the house. The list went on and on, but it boiled down to something very simple: Jill wanted Pat to pay attention to *her,* to really get to know her.

Pat realized that each item was a minor infraction, yet taken together they exposed him as an insensitive, uncaring husband. He hadn't intended to be, but he saw clearly that he indeed had been.

He was high with the discovery and eager to tell Jill about it, not sure how she would react. He was weepy and jittery because of lack of rest, and even though he had taken a giant step forward and knew he had settled accounts with God, he found it difficult to sleep.

Tuesday morning, December 21, he told Jill. "I know the only thing that's going to salvage this is a miracle, and I want you to know that the Lord has already performed a miracle in my heart and life. And I'm different. I know you've heard that from me a thousand times and there's no way I can ask you to believe me, but you will see it."

His heart was broken again as she didn't even honor him with a grunt. No response. No fight. No argument. No "Sure, Pat." No nothing. She could hardly function. She was expressionless. He was deeply worried about her. Scared. He knew he needed a plan of action, something concrete he could do to start proving that he meant business. When he had originally committed himself to Christ, even though he knew little about real growth until he seriously got into the Word, the commitment was for a lifetime, no turning back, no wavering, no doubting. When he'd committed himself to daily Scripture reading and study, he never missed a day. When he committed himself to memorizing a verse a day, he went at it with a passion, again never missing. When he committed himself to serious running, he worked his way up to six miles a day, every day, no matter where he was. When he committed himself to a health-food diet, he never wavered. And he had always been committed to an obsessive approach to his job, knowing as much as he could, covering all the bases, handling all the little things, giving everything for his owner, the boss, the team, the fans, the city. To him, commitment to something meant making a decision about it, closing the door, locking it, and throwing away the key.

Now he was ready to turn his sights on his marriage. He would commit himself to Jill with all that was in him for the glory of God and with the Lord's help, he prayed he would be successful. He felt he had lost everything, and he was now ready to work out of fear. He would attack that list and start ticking off the solutions to all those shortcomings, but he would never consider any of them fully solved. No, he would use that list until he had it memorized, turning it from a collection of negatives to a collection of positives, things that he would remember to do for the rest of his life.

The trouble now was that Jill was not receptive. He worried that he had pushed her beyond the point of no return. What if he did all this and still was not able to win her back? That became his first and primary goal. It would do him no good to be the best husband in the world if his wife no longer loved him or cared about their future.

Pat thought back on just the last few months and realized that indeed there had been a change. Had she given up? The fire was gone. The nagging. The yelling. And he had been blind enough to have enjoyed the peace. But if it had been a harbinger of fading love, of a dying ember, of a draining of emotion that could not be replaced, he would regret it for his whole life.

Wednesday night after work, it was the same story. Jill was a shell of her former self, unable to think, to move, to respond, to speak, to smile, to work, to do anything more than get the kids fed and dressed and herself stationed before the television. She couldn't even cry.

"The scary thing was," she said, "I didn't know if I was losing my mind or what. I saw my poor husband, begging for some semblance of what I used to be. He would have been thrilled even if I had yelled at him again. But there was nothing there. I looked as deep inside myself as I could see and there was no love, no emotion, no hatred, nothing. It wasn't as if I were even sad. I was nothing. Except scared. I knew that finally, after all these years, I had gotten his attention. And now I didn't want it. I heard him say, again, that he was different. Did I believe it? No, I had no reason to. The trouble was, I didn't care if it was true. Even if it was, it was too late. I was gone, over the brink. I felt nothing for him or for myself. Psychologically and emotionally dead? Without a doubt."

Pat told her about his list and his resolve once again. She wouldn't look at him. He burst into tears, trying to go on, trying to promise, to plead, to convince her of his sincerity, to prove that it was of God. "Come back, Jill," he managed, his voice thick, tears streaming down his face, "I want this right." It was as if she looked right through him.

Pat prayed silently most of the day, acknowledging that God would have to take a wrecking ball to the marriage, to destroy it so it could be rebuilt from the bottom up. He began to realize that that had already happened, or at best, it was happening right then with Jill unable to respond. Pat knew he couldn't rebuild the marriage without her. He sensed he had all the resolve and determination and heavenly ordination he could have wanted, but he was convinced that without Jill, nothing he did would be successful.

Jill had napped most of the afternoon, yet, even so was on her way to bed early. Pat struggled with his emotions, fighting the frustration over her not even looking at him, burning with regret that at times he had treated her the same way, though without the same reason. He took a deep breath and fought the tears. "Jill," he said, "I don't know what the outcome of this is going to be, but I know that God is going to use it one way or the other. It's either going to be a great success story, or it's going to be a devastating one. Someday I'm going to share it, either way. Either as someone who saw God miraculously transform the situation, or as one who failed and lost and has a warning for others."

Jill shook her head slowly and stared at the floor, her eyelids heavy. Lifelessly, dejectedly, she said, "Fine. Cool. Terrific. Sure, He can use it. Fine with me. He can use it for the world, but if He's not going to use it here, I don't care." And she trudged off to bed.

To Pat it was frightening and almost unbelievable. He felt he had nowhere else to turn. He was still too embarrassed to call friends or professionals. What would they think? They'd be shocked, disappointed. His pride was still a difficult barrier. A long-time collector of books, he had more than three thousand in the house and decided he had to find something that would help. Jill had bought dozens of books on marriage and family over the years, reading them and underlining them in red and leaving them where Pat could find them. To him they were froth, something for the little woman to concern herself with while he was digging through meaty commentaries. Now he looked for just that kind of book. Until midnight, he searched, reading a few paragraphs here, a table of contents there, a back cover, a chapter.

All he found downstairs were books that told wives how to treat their husbands right, in the hope that this would bring about the best in the husband. Jill had done the best she could with the man she had to work with, he decided. He needed something for himself, something that would expose him for what he was, give him hints on how to pick up the pieces and run with the new resolve he had received from God. He felt he was right with the Lord, that he had been forgiven. But when he had asked Jill's forgiveness, she looked the other way, unable to give it.

Dejected but not defeated, exhausted but not ready for sleep, Pat made his way upstairs and tiptoed into the darkened room. Jill slept soundly, if not peacefully. The depression had taken such a toll on her mind and body that she was drained. Judging by all the visible symptoms, it's possible she had suffered a nervous breakdown. She could have slept for hours, day and night. And often she did.

She didn't even stir when Pat dropped into bed on his back, on top of the blankets. He lay there, full of resolve but desperate for tangible help, and unable to sleep. At three o'clock in the morning he headed back downstairs, still searching, trying to wind down, hoping to get some sleep before another busy day. The team he'd helped build around Julius (Dr. J.) Erving now had Moses Malone at center, and the Sixers were the hot-

test team in pro sports. It would be a tumultuous year. He
knew they'd win the championship. *And if we do,* he realized,
*and if we're in a victory parade down Broad Street, I won't care.
I won't even want to be there unless Jill is beside me, enjoying it
as much as I am.*

Whipped, he went back upstairs to bed. Jill was still dead to
the world. This time he flipped on the light on his bedside
table. And there, on that little table, illuminated by the light,
was a book Jill had brought home from a women's Bible study
eight months before. It had rested there collecting dust. She
hadn't even read it, so it was unmarked, and apparently un-
opened. *Love-Life for Every Married Couple* (Zondervan, 1980)
by Ed Wheat, M.D., author of *Intended for Pleasure* (Revell,
1981).

Pat picked up the book carefully and slowly, hoping against
hope in his exhaustion that it wasn't a mirage. The cover blurb
read "How to fall in love, stay in love, rekindle your love." He
flipped the book over to find three endorsements from well-
known evangelicals, including Dr. James Dobson, but one
leapt out at him. Charles Swindoll had written: "I read everything I can get my hands on regarding marriage, the home, and
family relationships. But in all my reading, I know of nothing
better than Dr. Ed Wheat's book when it comes to the subject
of intimacy between husbands and their wives. It is biblical,
practical, specific, easily understood, and filled with hope."

Pat almost wept. A Swindoll endorsement meant a lot to him
because he was one of the California preacher's most ardent
followers. He had read every Swindoll book and listened to
him on the radio every day. Plus, just the way Swindoll worded
it: *Hope* he needed. *Easy to understand* was mandatory in the
condition he found himself. *Specific,* oh yes. *Practical,* please.
Biblical, of course. He so badly needed what this book promised that he began reading it right then, reading as far as he
could until he slept, underlining and recognizing himself on
every page.

"Every page was convicting," he recalls. "I read it every
night for weeks, reading and rereading, dog-earing my copy

until it looked as if it'd gone through a war. I was embarrassed as I read of husbands who got marriage out of the way as a customary obligation and then got back to the business of running their lives. 'That's me,' I'd write, and 'Typical,' or 'Guilty.' "

The hope, the life, the water for this husband dying of thirst was the central theme that called to him from the pages: If just one partner cares, that's all it takes. The marriage can be resuscitated. The love can be rekindled. The relationship can be resurrected if the biblical principles are followed. All it takes is one partner to care, to try, to work at it.

Pat knew Jill was in no condition to help. He was going to have to be that one. He was willing, whether she was ready or not. He pored through the Wheat book, desperate to get Jill's attention, to do anything to win her back and get his marriage on its feet. Already he had set the tone for the rest of his life. He was going to make his marriage his top priority. He cared about it more than anything else in the world. Now that he was finally running one of the best teams in any sport, a goal he had pursued for his whole career, it paled in comparison to the urgency of this task. The competitor in Pat surged to the fore. He would battle for his wife with ten times the intensity he would put into a ball game.

Reading every chance he got, praying fervently throughout the day, Pat saw God begin to work almost immediately. There was no thawing in Jill, but two "coincidences" worked together in Pat's life that only God could have engineered. And they both occurred Wednesday, December 22, 1982.

Chapter Twelve

Commitment

Jill wasn't trying to punish Pat. She could see he was scared stiff, desperate to reach her. In fact, if she felt any emotion, it was pity. She had no guarantees that his resolve would last, but she quickly stopped doubting his sincerity. She was in a fog, trapped, unable to function normally. Clearly he was trying. Clearly she had his full attention for the first time in ten years. But she felt no love for him.

They were both putting on a front for the sake of the children. Jill wouldn't look at Pat. Pat couldn't take his eyes off her. He was looking for a break, a change, a difference, some hint, some clue of a thawing. He could have been angry with her for not responding, but somehow he knew this was no ordinary silent treatment. The woman was in trouble, and that meant nothing but bad news for him.

Pat prayed constantly, begging God to work in her life the way He had worked in his. Daily he renewed his vow to make her his top priority. Now he just wanted a chance to make it mean something. He didn't want it to be in vain, but he needed strength to continue when there was no encouragement coming his way.

Jill was afraid that she might have to be hospitalized. She had no more idea about the future of the marriage or her sanity than Pat did. If only she could have said, "Bear with me. I'll get over this. It's temporary." But she had less hope than he did, and his was hanging by a thread.

His daily phone call was still a ritual, but now he couldn't weasel an "I love you" out of her no matter what he said. When he hung up he would sit at his desk and cry, hoping to be able to compose himself before he had to face anyone.

When he left the house in the morning he talked to Jill as to a child, telling her that he was going to work, that he was a new man, and that she would soon see that he was serious. "I understand now, I see where I was wrong, and I'm changing. I've turned over a new leaf for real this time, with God's help. You may not believe me, and that's fine. I'm just going to prove it to you, that's all, if it takes the rest of my life."

The Wheat book had been encouraging Pat to do these things because they were right—the same reason why he should have been doing them all along. These were principles Dr. Wheat had drawn straight from the Bible. Pat was not to smother her with kindness and consideration just to get a response. And Dr. Wheat recommended not telling her that he was even reading the book or that he had a specific plan.

"Watch me, Jill, because I'm serious this time, and I'm working at it day and night. I can't sleep, I can't think of anything else. I'll never give up."

Jill was speaking quietly and calmly, more so than ever before in her marriage. "All right," she would say. "You can do what you want, but I don't feel anything right now and I can't say I ever will. Don't expect anything from me and don't tell me what to do. I'm through faking it. I'm tired of it."

"I was so neutral, it scared me," she says. "It was like looking down on myself as if I were someone else."

Wednesday, December 22, was the day the office staff had their version of the Christmas party the players and their families had already had Sunday night. On the way Pat wondered when he would be able to get a decent night's sleep. His emotions were on edge, and he felt a weight on his back and shoulders that would take a week to sleep off.

He knew he had to put on a big front for the office staff, all of whom ultimately reported to him. The party had been planned for weeks and several prizes had been worked out with various firms so several people could win something very special. In fact, the top three prizes were very expensive; one, a weekend to Disney World, all expenses paid.

A half-dozen pizzas were delivered, and there were songs and crazy games. But everyone was looking forward to the big drawing. All their names had been put into a hat and swished around. Finally the moment came for the big drawing. Rather than giving the top three gifts to the first three names drawn, they played it so that the first name got the smallest prize, a gag gift, and each succeeding name received a better gift. The last name drawn would win the trip to Disney World and the Epcot Center in Florida.

Pat enjoyed the frivolity as much as a man could in his position. But he did find himself glancing at his watch more than once. Before going home, he had to pick up a turkey for Saturday's Christmas dinner. He knew it would be getting dark early, and it was already an ugly gray day. And being that close to Christmas, there would probably be a crowd at the turkey farm.

Finally, the drawing was down to the last three names. Someone won a very nice radio. The second to last person won a combination radio and tape player. "And now the winner of the big trip for two, all expenses paid. Drum roll, please!" Everyone groaned and begged to know. "Pat Williams!"

Pat was stunned. He made a crack as he stepped forward to receive the prize, but as soon as he turned away from the crowd, he broke down. He sensed immediately that this crazy drawing, this unusual prize, was God's way of helping him start on his list of priorities for Jill. They would spend the last weekend of January alone, together, in Florida. During the season. He'd show her where his priorities lay. "Thank you, Lord."

He hurried to the car and drove to the turkey farm. The sky was nearly black as he stood in a long line of people eager to pick up their Christmas dinner fare. Pat's hands were thrust deep into the pockets of his coat as he stared straight ahead, thinking, praying, worrying about the wife who was undoubtedly immobile before the TV again, and all the while also marveling over the immediate encouragement he had just received.

But what was this? In front of him was a young couple, the man with a baby in his arms. When the young father transferred the tiny one to his shoulder, and the infant peeked out at Pat from his mountain of blankets, Pat realized it was an Asian child. Pat's throat tightened and his eyes filled. He pressed his lips together and stared at the ground, then back at the Oriental baby. He pushed a hand up under his glasses as the tears came. "Lord, what's happening?"

Inaudibly, he felt God impress upon his heart, "That baby is not here by accident. It's no coincidence that you just happened to get here at this time and wind up standing behind this couple at this farm."

Pat said to himself, "I know. I know."

He wiped his face clean, swallowed, and took a deep breath. "How old's the baby?" The couple turned around, beaming, eager to talk about their first child. He was a Korean orphan and they had just recently adopted him through the Holt Agency. "My wife's been after me to do that for years," Pat said.

They told him it was a little expensive with all the fees and that there was an agonizing wait, but that otherwise it was relatively easy if you qualified. "You folks from around here?" Pat asked.

"Moorestown."

He laughed. "You're kidding! That's where we live."

When he got home he burst into the house. "Jill, you'll never guess what happened today."

"I don't want to guess. Just tell me."

"We had a big drawing at the party for a trip to Orlando for two, all expenses paid, to Disney World and Epcot Center."

"Yeah?"

"Guess who won? You'll never guess."

"You're right, I won't. I told you I don't want to guess. If you want to tell me, tell me."

"Pat Williams!"

"You?"

"You got it. We can go. It'll be in January, during the season. Won't it be great?"

She shrugged.

"Don't you want to go with me?"

"Sure, why not?"

Jill thought it was almost funny that they won a romantic weekend for two during the lowest point in their marriage. "I honestly felt that I'd rather go with someone else," she says. "I was kind enough not to say that, but I was in fact dreading the trip. I didn't want to be mean, but I didn't want to be alone with him for a weekend. I knew he was trying, but he wasn't reaching me. It was as if I were living out the old sports cliche, 'I'm rooting for you but betting against you.' "

"You'll never guess what else happened."

She just stared at him.

"At the turkey farm."

Still nothing.

"I wind up in line right behind a couple named Burkheimer, and they've got a Korean orphan."

"So?"

"They're from right here in Moorestown. I'm gonna call 'em and see if we can go over. I want you to see the baby. You want to?"

"Right now? Not really."

"Come on, I'm gonna call 'em."

The whole family visited the Burkheimers, and Jill busied herself with her own kids to keep from having to interact too much. She playacted wonderfully, bringing a little gift for the mother and surviving all the social amenities. Pat carried the conversation and Jill jabbered with the children about how cute the baby was and wasn't he tiny. She didn't know what to make of Pat's sudden craziness over something she had wanted for years. Could she get excited about it? She didn't even want to think about another mouth to feed in a house where she felt like a zombie. But Pat wouldn't be deterred. The next day he phoned the Holt Agency and asked them to air mail an application and any other material he might need.

He tried to be as animated as possible over the holidays, but he was getting a very cold shoulder from Jill. He was genuinely excited about the two Wednesday events and hoped Jill could see that it was because he was so committed to pleasing her. But all he got out of her that night was that she wondered what her life might have been like if she had married the guy she was going with before she met Pat.

"My life probably would have been a lot different, and a lot happier."

Pat was crushed, broken. He didn't need that right then. The cold, silent treatment was better than that. Somehow he knew she hadn't meant to hurt him. That made it even worse. He knew she was merely telling the truth, expressing how she felt. She really meant it. She hated her life, her marriage, and—he feared—her husband.

His mother joined them for a few days beginning December 23. Jill hid her problem well from her mother-in-law. But she wouldn't look at Pat, would speak to him only when spoken to, and then only if his mother was present.

When Jill woke up on Christmas morning, the house was alive with the sounds of kids who couldn't wait to open presents. Pat was propped up on one elbow, staring into her eyes. "Merry Christmas," he said.

Hardly, she thought.

"Tell me what you're thinking right now," he suggested, hoping maybe six days of effort, a visitor in the house, the special nature of the day, and the thought of the children's imminent joy might have had an impact.

"I'm thinking I'd rather be any place in the world than here today."

Pat couldn't have been lower. He wanted to ram his fist through the window, shout at her, shake her, cry, plead, crawl, whatever was necessary. How could she say that? How could she mean it? Pat knew God had dealt with him, that he had been broken and forgiven. He knew in his heart he was different. But it wasn't working. As she slowly began a monologue, questioning why she ever married him, what the reasons were, and why she had no business doing it, he had to leave the room.

He was at his best with his mother and the kids, and by the time Jill joined them to open presents, she was ready with her phony happy face, fooling everyone perfectly. Everyone but Pat. To him she was cold, a wall. She didn't look at him, listen to him, or even answer him unless he specifically put a question to her. "Isn't that nice, Jill? What do you think of that?"

"Um-hm," she'd say, and immediately find a reason to talk to one of the kids.

Pat absolutely bowled her over with gifts. She got more things from him than ever, and rather than the impersonal gifts she was used to getting, like a CB radio, it was clear he had put some thought and creativity into these. Nothing general like perfume or jewelry. No, these were personal things, clothes and special surprises. It all culminated in a trail of clues that led her all over the house and out into the yard and finally to the front bushes, where he had hidden a moped.

The kids, who had known all along, were ecstatic with the hunt. Jill pretended to enjoy it, and when she discovered the moped, a hint of a smile cracked her face for the first time in a week. Pat needed that to keep going. Through the pages Pat had been drinking in during sleepless nights, Dr. Wheat had been admonishing the devoted spouse to be patient. If it takes years, so be it. Do it because it's right, not just so everything will be cured immediately. But fast action was what Pat wanted.

Don't blow it. Don't go too fast. Don't expect too much too soon. Pat had read it and he knew it, but it was becoming very, very difficult. "It was a weird feeling," he remembers. "Like living with and courting an absolute stranger, a person I'd never seen before. Someone off the street would have been more responsive."

He wanted and needed something, but he was getting nothing. Nothing but that hint of a smile when Jill, without looking at him, thanked him for the little motorbike. Had he known what she was thinking, he might have been defeated.

She had faked the smile, yet it was all that would keep him going for the next week. She wondered what in the world she was going to do with a moped in New Jersey in the dead of winter with three kids to take care of. She wondered if he was now trying to buy her off. And that simply wouldn't work. Not because she chose not to let it, but because that wouldn't create real feelings in her. And except for that smile, with which she had surprised even herself, she wasn't going to pretend there was anything inside that wasn't really there.

Over the holidays the Williamses hosted more guests, and on New Year's Jill played the perfect hostess for fifty. But when they were gone and it was just her and Pat and the children, she was back in the pits, unresponsive to a husband who was weeping when he tried to talk to her, reading a book through and through, unable to sleep, and looking scared.

Pat was nearly losing hope that he would have any impact on Jill. But when he reached chapter thirteen in Dr. Wheat's book, "Prescription for a Superb Marriage," he decided to simply settle in, make it his memorized guideline, and go for broke. More than anything else, he wanted to win Jill back, but he wasn't even going to think about that for the time being. He couldn't. It was too painful.

All he could do was one thing at a time, and that one thing was to give his wife the best, not in some generic sense, but in a carefully prescribed plan as outlined by Dr. Ed Wheat. Pat was ready to put it into practice for as long as was necessary, simply because it was right.

Chapter Thirteen

Toward Long-Term Healing

Dr. Wheat called his prescription for a superb marriage a practical course of action "that is both uncomplicated and effective." He entitled it BEST because that was the acronym formed by what he called "four positive elements that will transform any marriage: Blessing, Edifying, Sharing, and Touching."

Author Wheat made clear that these measures were to be implemented simultaneously, and—of particular appeal to Pat—they could be implemented by one partner alone. It was like a breath of fresh air to read that "in many cases, one of you will have to make the first move without any promise of cooperation from the other."

It was here that the light came on and everything Pat had been reading came into focus. "It became obvious to me," he says, "that just as when you're putting together an athletic team or honing and developing a skill, the fundamentals have to be mastered first. The fundamentals of being a good partner had been missing from the very beginning of our marriage, especially in me, but also in her, despite the wonderful example her parents had been. In talking with other couples, I'm now finding that this is a widespread problem, even in marriages that have not deteriorated as far as ours had."

Dr. Wheat, of course, carefully elucidates his points in a lengthy treatment in his own book, and the Williamses highly recommend it for careful study. He even provides brief biblical word studies, and uses case histories, anecdotes, and medical facts to make his point. From Pat's perspective, however, here is what he gleaned from the material for application in his own marriage.

Blessing

Pat felt challenged to first *bless* Jill in four specific ways:

1. *To speak well* of her and respond with good words in every situation. Speaking well of her, to Pat, meant praising her to others, something he had on his list, which she had been hammering at for years. "Jill had a real problem with that, but really it was my problem. I just couldn't bring myself to do it. Maybe I thought it was a little sissified because I'd been teased about girlfriends. Maybe I thought it was like holding hands or kissing in public, making yourself vulnerable, losing your independence."

For some reason, Jill had never had a problem praising Pat to others. She would gladly tell people that she thought he was the best speaker she'd ever heard. That embarrassed him a little, but she did it anyway. Pat told Jill, privately, that she was his favorite singer, "But I was afraid maybe it would sound like bragging if I told other people that."

Pat was almost afraid to start. It was not a natural reaction for him. But she needed it, longed for it. They'd had many an argument over just that, but Pat had never really realized how important it was to her. He would say, "Jill, you're telling me the whole evening was ruined because I didn't compliment you before dinner?"

"You had the perfect opportunity. Why didn't you?"

Now, having vowed to do whatever was necessary to win her back, Pat was determined to begin at the first opportunity.

Related to that first point under blessing one's mate was speaking kind words *to her* as well. No matter how difficult and testy and uncomfortable the situation, Pat knew he had to respond to her kindly. Not easy. Many times their exchanges had been cross. There was an edge to his voice that upset her, agitated her even more. "There were countless times, I realize now, that I would have been so much better off if I had said just one less paragraph, one less sentence, one less word. And all the while, when I was just putting our arguments out of my mind, they were taking their toll on Jill and building to a devastating conclusion, unbeknown to me. Learning to be silent or respond kindly was a hard lesson for me, but it had been a great failing of mine."

Pat now recommends a ninety-day test wherever he goes. It is to be applied to one's mate, children, and everyone else with whom one comes into contact. "You must go ninety straight days," he says, "during which you respond with kind, uplifting, encouraging words to everything that comes your way, good or bad. If you blow it, you start over at day one and shoot for ninety again."

2. *To do kind things.* It's no more than the golden rule. Pat wanted to remind himself constantly of this by always asking, "What can I do now that will be a kind act for Jill?" The first thing that came to mind was the fact that Jill loved freshly squeezed orange juice in the morning.

The next morning, Pat got up and stiffly went down to the kitchen. "They say M & Ms won't melt in your hand. In our house in December ice cubes won't either!" He squeezed her a glass of orange juice and left it on her nightstand.

There was no response. Not that day, not the next, when he did it again. Or the next. Or the next. But it was a kind thing he thought of to do and he's been doing it every day since then, no matter where they are. Sometimes she prefers herbal tea or a natural milkshake, but Pat's first deed every morning is to treat her to something he prepares himself.

Eventually, of course, that simple act was one of the things that began slowly to break into Jill's injured soul. At first she questioned it, wondered at his motives, wondered how long it would last, didn't want to encourage him or imply any hope. Even today—though the feeling is rarer all the time—Jill sometimes fears that the whole thing is going to end, that Pat will have finally crossed everything off his list, will decide he's done his duty, and will revert to the same person he was in 1982.

Pat, not smugly, has no such fear. "Why would I want to go back there?" he reasons. "Without knowing it, I was on a barren, parched desert island. I was starving to death. Now I realize what I was missing, and I enjoy what a good marriage is all about."

3. *To express thankfulness and appreciation verbally.* That was always a sore spot with Jill and a hard thing for Pat to do when he did occasionally notice something that deserved such a response. "It wasn't intentional," he says. "In fact, there were times when I did notice some of her work or creativity and planned to mention it, but just forgot. The only way to cure that was to tune out the rest of the world, the job, and the happenings of the day when I got home and make noticing her handiwork a priority. When she had to point out things she'd done, it took all the joy out of it for her."

4. *To pray for her good and the highest blessing of God in her life.* It suddenly dawned on Pat that though he had developed a disciplined prayer life for the first time, praying for Baseball Chapel, athletes' salvation, and missionary efforts around the world, he really hadn't been praying for his wife on a regular basis.

He put a little sign near his office phone that asked, "Have you prayed for Jill today?" He found praying for her throughout the day helped create a spiritual bond that had never been there before.

Dr. Wheat made the point that blessing should always be the response, no matter what the treatment from the spouse. No matter if she was nasty, sarcastic, indifferent, or emotionally dead. Pat's job was to create an atmosphere of peace by starting a new foundation, the first level of support for which was Blessing.

First Peter 3:7-9 were key verses to Dr. Wheat, and thus to Pat as he studied: "You husbands likewise, live with your wives in an understanding way, as with a weaker vessel, since she is a woman; and grant her honor as a fellow-heir of the grace of life, so that your prayers may not be hindered. To sum up, let all be harmonious, sympathetic, brotherly, kind-hearted, and humble in spirit; not returning evil for evil, or insult for insult, but giving a blessing instead; for you were called for the very purpose that you might inherit a blessing" (NAS).

An aspect of Dr. Wheat's counsel that Pat found especially helpful was an admonition to treat his wife as a guest in the home. He'd never thought of it, but so often the guest is the one treated with the highest esteem. Dr. Wheat encourages Christian husbands to first treat their wives and children as fellow Christians. It's now something Pat tries to practice every day.

He also tries to establish a climate that allows Jill and the kids to live to their fullest potential, something Dr. Wheat calls setting the thermostat.

Edifying

This is a word Pat had heard in church often but never really knew the meaning of. From Dr. Wheat's book he learned that it means to support or build up. Pat realized that the only way to praise Jill was frequently. "She was starved for it, as most women are. She had a good sense of humor and always seemed able to take my teasing and needling, but the criticism was also constant, and it was crushing."

Pat realized that Jill had very little confidence in herself, despite her beauty and her gifts. In many ways, she thought she was worthless. He wanted to build her up, support her, develop inner strengthening through praising and complimenting her.

Pat remains amazed that a woman with as much going for her as Jill has a self-image problem, yet the validity of such an attitude is borne out in interviews with such superstar beauties as Brooke Shields. Here is a young woman who is the heart-throb of many men and the envy of just as many women, yet she tells interviewers that she constantly worries about being too fat, too awkward, too tall, too this, too that. Apparently, it's not false modesty.

Another part of edifying is to establish peace and harmony.

One of the keys is studying one's partner. A complaint Jill had made through the years was that Pat never really knew her. "I wish you'd study me the way you study your owner when you're about to hit him up for a couple of million dollars to sign a player. You pick the time of day he's going to be in the best mood, and you have your pitch all worked out. But you don't know me. You don't study me. You don't really know who I am."

Proverbs 24:3, 4 are the key verses: "Through wisdom is an house builded; and by understanding it is established: And by knowledge shall the chambers be filled with all precious and pleasant riches" (KJV).

In his excellent book *Strike the Original Match,* Chuck Swindoll expands on these two key verses. First, a marriage is *built* by *wisdom. Wisdom* has the idea of "seeing with discernment," while *built* means "to restore or rebuild something so that it flourishes." Pat sensed his marriage would flourish and grow if he treated Jill with discernment, and dug underneath the surface to the depths of her mind and soul.

Second, a marriage is *established* by *understanding.* When husbands respond to wives with a high degree of insight and sensitivity, marriages can be corrected and put in order. When we use wisdom, no longer is it necessary to take conflicts and irritations personally, but we can see them from God's vantage point as being either good or essential for our further growth.

Third, a marriage is *filled to overflowing* by *knowledge* and *perception.* Every area of the marriage relationship will overflow in abundance if we carefully study, probe, discover and learn from all failures and successes. A teachable, open, non-defensive spirit is required, however.

Wisdom, understanding, and knowledge come only from the Lord. God must be the Lord of our lives and marriages. Proverbs 2:6 says, "For the Lord gives wisdom; From His mouth come knowledge and understanding" (NAS).

Pat wanted wisdom, understanding, and knowledge, and he set about studying Jill by listening to her. Since she wasn't saying much just then, he had to go back to the list God had helped him put together from her past statements. "It occurred to me that the most fun we'd had in our relationship was during the summer of '72 when we were courting, expressing our love, and heading toward marriage."

Pat had been under the mistaken assumption that once the knot was tied, you settle in and grind it out for the rest of your married life. Why spend more time working on something that's already done? Why reinvent the wheel? "There were high points and good times, of course, but I thought it could never be as good as those days during the engagement period. However, I was wrong, and I felt Dr. Wheat's book had opened a very special door of enlightenment for me."

Sharing

Dr. Wheat's challenge was to share time, activity, interests, concerns, ideas, innermost thoughts, spiritual walk, family objectives, and career goals. "Jill had been so frustrated by my inability to give of myself, to listen to her uninterrupted. I now wanted to develop a sensitive awareness between us."

Along with that, Dr. Wheat laid heavy emphasis on going to bed and getting up together. Pat knew he was just flat guilty. Many nights Jill had confronted him about that, begging him to not make her go to sleep alone. But he countered, "What am I to do, Jill? I have to watch this game." Or, "I'm not through studying and I don't want to let this lapse."

How does a woman argue with Bible study? She knew it was important, but the clear, subliminal message she was getting was that his job and his Bible study were more important than she was. When she was particularly upset, he might walk her upstairs, sit on the bed and talk with her, kiss her good night, turn the light off, and then rush back down to his responsibilities. "If I need the extra hour for my duties, then I need it," he rationalized.

Little did he know that many nights Jill wasn't confronting him. She was simply, sadly going to bed alone, forlorn, forsaken, frustrated. And she'd cry herself to sleep.

Pat's attitude about that carried over into other areas of family life. He didn't have time to sit and touch her and talk to her.

And if she dragged him away from Philadelphia for a weekend in the mountains with the kids, he "needed" to be on the phone half the day and found reasons to have to get back early. "I'd go crackers if I had to be away for more than two days."

"You think the whole NBA would disintegrate without you," Jill would charge.

"In a way, I did. I had always had my hand on the throttle, and I never took a break. I didn't know about the rest of the league, but I certainly wasn't going to be responsible for the Sixers losing the edge because I had missed something. Again, Jill got the message loud and clear. The team was all-important. She was already owned and taken care of."

"Therefore shall a man leave his father and his mother, and shall cleave unto his wife; and they shall be one flesh." In the Bible, *cleave* describes the skin that clings to the body's bones, the tongue that sticks to the roof of a dry mouth, and attachment of scales to a fish. Dr. Wheat further explained *cleave* in the original Hebrew as a word that is similar to the action of bonding two pieces of wood together—so securely that to break the bond would destroy both pieces of wood. Chuck Swindoll has stated, "When a man marries a woman he is to literally glue himself to her. Their relationship is meant to be forever; it's not designed to be terminable. It's a permanent relationship which requires constant time and attention."

Pat and Jill have broken Genesis 2:24 down to three simple words: leave, cleave, and weave. Until then, Pat had only left.

Touching

Pat knew he had reached the zenith of Dr. Wheat's counsel when he read this qualifier: ". . . even though you apply every other principle I have given you in this book, it will be of little avail unless you learn to touch each other often and joyfully in nonsexual ways. Physical contact is absolutely essential. . . ."

Pat found that a powerful statement and realized it was another of his weak areas. How many times had Jill told him he touched her only when he wanted something? Yet Dr. Wheat was saying that a tender touch tells your wife that she's cared for. It calms her fears, it soothes pain, it brings comfort, it gives emotional security—the one thing Jill was most barren of right then.

Dr. Wheat believes that American society is so sex conscious because people are really looking for the intimacy that has been lost through the nonacceptance of touching relationships. Only handshakes, contact sports, or sex are acceptable for males, but the most important one is neglected or scorned or ridiculed and certainly not endorsed by Madison Avenue.

Pat studied Dr. Wheat's twenty-five tips on nonsexual touching, and took a lesson from the teenage couples he's noticed. They sit close in church, in the car, in front of the TV. There is a lot of eye contact. Pat began applying nonsexual touching in large doses. In return he got nothing. Jill wasn't pulling away, but neither was she responding. Yet he knew that an hour of touching wasn't going to cure a decade of neglect. He just hung in there and continued in spite of the lack of response.

Pat emphasizes that "none of this is ever mastered. It takes constant work and concentration, especially for men in jobs like mine where the work isn't over at the end of eight hours. You have to go at this like a recovering alcoholic, one day at a time. It's not automatic, but a daily battle. It's no easier today than it was two years ago. You just have to do it. It's hard work, but it pays dividends."

Pat feels that if he concentrates on three areas of B-E-S-T and forgets a fourth, he'll have trouble.

By this time, Jill was aware that Pat was reading the book and had a list he was intently working at. "He told me he was not going to tell me how to respond. I told him that was good, because I didn't want to be told and I still wasn't promising anything. When he showed me the list, I agreed that, yes, these are the things I raised over the years. But I noticed he had crossed some of them out already and I worried that maybe he was doing this for his own ego. He was going to enjoy a major accomplishment if he could eventually tick all the items off. Then he would be a successful husband and that would be the end of it. We both cried a lot over the next several days, which was the first emotion I had felt for a while."

Jill admits she was grateful he was trying, but she was scared that she would wake up the next morning and everything would be back the way it was two weeks before. Worse, she knew that her lack of response to his sincere effort could be one of the causes of that. But there was nothing she could do. She would be cordial and try to stop being so cynical. But she would not fake feelings. And there still were none.

Pat and Jill had agreed to speak and sing at a church in Philadelphia on New Year's eve, but they had received from friends Paul and Connie Beals a gift certificate for dinner first at the finest restaurant in South Jersey. Pat asked Jill if she would join him—as if he were asking for a first date. "I was scared. What if she said no?"

In fact, she said something—not really negatively—about having to eat somewhere anyway. Pat was nervous, careful. He treated her like a date, and wonder of wonders, she was cordial. That was a step. He enjoyed the evening. They communicated. Not about themselves, or their problem, but they were talking. And the New Year's eve service went well.

Meanwhile, Pat was still poring over the Wheat book, and the freshly squeezed orange juice was coming every day. "I'm heaping on double doses of Blessing, Edifying, Sharing, and Touching. Still no response."

Fifty people had been invited to enjoy New Year's Day at the Williamses. Pat was hoping that after the nice dinner the night before and the rewarding ministry partnership they had shared, maybe things would be warmer and friendlier the next day. But no. Jill was cold and distant again. "Each day was absolutely different," Pat says. "There was no predicting. Jill kept reminding me that she hadn't promised anything, that she didn't want to be pushed, that she didn't want me making any assumptions. I was impatient. I wanted her back, and I wanted to know when that had been accomplished."

The Sixers were playing the Lakers in Philadelphia on the first Wednesday in January, and for the first time ever, Pat came home late in the afternoon. He surprised Jill by stopping in to see Karyn and Bobby at their gymnastics class, and ate at home.

"I just had to talk to Jill, game night or not. I had sensed during the day that one of the things that still had to be bothering her was guilt and remorse over her life-style during the last half of 1982. Self-acceptance after that would be difficult. I knew I had caused it, but she had to be feeling low about not having been an ideal wife and mother and person during those months; and I wanted to assure her that I understood and that she could know she was forgiven."

Pat examined his motives and his plan of attack, knowing that Jill couldn't articulate those feelings even if she was aware of them, and that he would have to carry the ball. But he didn't want to come off parental or like a know-it-all, and certainly not holier-than-thou. In fact, he hit her right where she lived. He sat her down and, gently holding her hands, told her he thought he might know some of the things she was feeling. Her torrent of tears told him he was right.

"Jill," he concluded, "I want you to know that I don't care anything about that. I know my actions forced you to do things you weren't comfortable with and that you were looking for something outside the home that you should have found in me. So, I understand and I forgive you, and I take the responsibility."

Suddenly it was six-thirty and the game was starting in an hour. Pat had a half-hour drive through traffic. For the first time in two and a half weeks, he saw some life, some animation in her face, something in her eyes. He'd been right, she'd appreciated it, even if she couldn't say it. As he was leaving, she said, "Boy, I wish I could go to the game with you tonight."

Of course she couldn't get a sitter at the last minute, but Pat's heart leapt. "It was as if I felt a burst of energy inside. That was a critical night. I needed it to keep going. It would still be a long haul, but I had been desperate for a signal. And now I had one."

Chapter Fourteen

Rekindled

Pat felt high. He felt good. He felt hope for the first time since the slight smile in the front yard at Christmas. He called her at half-time of the game and she was more than cordial. Though Jill admits she still had a long way to go and wouldn't have necessarily pointed to that day as a turning point, Pat definitely does.

"From that night on, I remember each day getting a little better. Again, there were inconsistencies and sometimes it would seem we were back to square one, but I was motivated to keep going, without pushing her, to the point where we would build a new life together."

For the first time in his married life, probably for the first time since the Miss Illinois Pageant nearly ten years before, Pat realized he had fallen in love with his wife. "I was absolutely out of control in love with her. I started spending like there was no tomorrow, showering her with gifts and cards and notes and flowers."

The more he saw results—just little things at first, the squeeze of a hand, an embrace returned, a hint of a smile, a look full in the face—the more he continued the onslaught of blessing, edifying, sharing, and touching. "I was like a giddy teenager. I could see this corpse of a woman, this woman who had been unable to even move, let alone smile or respond in any way, coming to life. Admittedly, there were still times when she reminded me not to push it, not to rush or force her. She still didn't want to be told how I expected her to react in any specific ways." Every now and then Pat's enthusiasm would cause him to slip, to ask for a response, but "as long as I wasn't overbearing, we were okay."

During the first weekend in January, Pat surprised Jill by packing a bag for her and having a limousine pick her up before a game and take them to the Franklin Plaza Hotel afterward. Jill was shocked. Pat was trying to prove he could be creative with her. They had a lovely late dinner, and the next day he not only took her shopping, but also to lunch.

They spent a wonderful weekend and enjoyed each other physically for the first time since early December. Of course, their sexual relationship had been nonexistent during this difficult time, which was a great frustration for Pat. He assumed that its resumption might be the signal of the breaking down of the barrier that existed between them, but he was afraid to initiate anything. She became very cold whenever any gesture or caress seemed to have any sexual overtones. Most disconcerting of all was that even now when their physical relationship did seem to be getting back to normal, Pat found Jill feeling pushed again the next time.

He had thought that once they were together again physically, everything would be easy going after that. But in fact, overnight Jill could revert to the distant, depressed, cold woman who would just as soon be anyone else's or no one's wife and anywhere else in the world but at home with Pat. "Don't rush me. Don't hurry me. I'm not ready."

Pat was thinking, *Not ready? Why not?* But Dr. Wheat's advice was ringing in his ear: "You can ruin a month's worth of careful work if you open your mouth too much or too soon and say something wrong."

Jill admits that by this time "every once in a while there was a flicker that he was getting to me. I wouldn't say it, but I knew he was trying. It was sinking in. I knew if I wasn't careful, he could get next to me, but I was still afraid I'd be hurt again."

Pat felt he needed to talk to Dr. Wheat personally, so he

phoned his office in Springdale, Arkansas. Dr. Wheat was not easy to get to, but when Pat reached him he quickly filled him in on the whole story and thanked him for the part his book had played so far. "I could tell he was thrilled," Pat recalls. "But I didn't tell him my name for fear he might be a basketball fan and would know me."

He said, "Dr. Wheat, I have to ask you. Why did it take me ten years to discover this? Why ten years? I'm just now finding out about this."

"Three basic reasons," Dr. Wheat said in a slow and deliberate manner. "We men are very, very slow learners, very stubborn, and very selfish. Be grateful you found out. Most men never do, or if they do, it's too late."

"Well, sir, I've got one more problem. The way I feel now, the way I'm going, I'm in such an intense love relationship with my wife that I'm afraid I'm going to burn out. Sometimes I wonder if I can last the weekend. When's all this going to end?"

"Listen, young man, God never intended it to end. God's design for every Christian marriage is that this intense romantic relationship will increase in intensity every day for the rest of your life. It's never going to end as long as you bless, edify, share with, and touch her."

Pat chuckled. "I don't know if I can take it," he told the doctor.

From that point on, it was a matter of Pat's applying the principles on a daily basis and Jill slowly but surely learning to respond. Pat became obsessed with the idea that they have another child, even with their application to the Holt Agency for a Korean orphan. "I don't deny that I thought a Korean orphan would tie us together more," he says, "and I wanted another child of our own because I felt we had a new relationship, a new marriage. And I wanted a child born of that. Eventually we decided to do both, not knowing that if she got pregnant it would eliminate the possibility of our adopting. That was just one of their rules."

Jill and Pat were going to the games together, going out together, and he was being creative. For her birthday he led her on another wild goose chase to find her present, a fur coat she had always wanted.

She still wasn't at the point where she could respond by running up to him and throwing her arms around him. "I was trying to help by saying the right things, and I knew he was trying so hard that I felt sorry for him. I hadn't resolved not to respond. I just couldn't. I was still afraid it would end, and I didn't want to be vulnerable, but I did try to offer a little encouragement."

Even the next weekend when they went to a cold Orlando for the trip to Disney World, they tried not to talk too much about their own situation because it was still an emotional sore spot. Jill had to admit the man was working. Two weekends in a row away from the team! Something was coming from him that had obviously been very deeply hidden for years.

One night late in January he came home, greeted everyone, and sat down for dinner. A smile played at his lips as he sat for over an hour waiting to see if anyone noticed. Finally, after another half-hour, Pat said, "Hey, Jilly, I thought I was the oblivious one. Don't you notice anything?"

She looked him up and down and shook her head. He got up and moved around. "Nothing different about your husband of a decade? Do I always come home looking like this?" She found a gray hair. "No! That's not it. Come on, gaze into my eyes and tell me what you see."

"Same color as always," she said, smiling. "What in the world are you up to?"

"You really don't know?"

"No!"

"You really can't tell anything different about me after seeing me come home every night for ten years with glasses?"

"Contacts! You've got contacts!"

Within a few days Pat came home with some more surprises. He bought a pair of cowboy boots, some sports shirts, and a couple of cardigan sweaters. He also filled his closet at work with shoe polish and brushes to start another ritual he had let slide sometime after getting married. Jill was starting to get the message.

Pat knew Sandi Patti was one of Jill's favorite gospel

recording artists, so one day he purchased the new tape, *Sandi's Song*, and left it on the seat in Jill's van. When they listened to it later, one cut, "You Never Gave Up on Me," became a theme song of their marriage, a tune that always incites emotion when they hear it now:

"You never gave up on me. When I was lost, you came and found me. You never gave up on me. Your lovin' arms came to surround me. You never gave up on me. I was drowning in a troubled sea. Lord, I'm so glad that you never gave up on me.

"I thought I had my life together, never bothered much to talk to you. Then I hit some stormy weather. Jesus you saw me through.

"You never gave up on me. When I said I wouldn't serve you, you never gave up on me. Lord, I really don't deserve you. You never gave up on me. You gave your life to set me free. I'm so glad that you never gave up on me."*

Late in January, Pat felt the need to call Jill's parents separately and to explain the whole situation, asking their forgiveness for the way he had treated their daughter through the years. Those were difficult, emotional calls but will remain a sweet memory for all three of them. "I felt God wanted me to do that, and until I did it, I knew things would never be really right."

The Holt Agency papers arrived early in 1983 too, and Pat and Jill went to a meeting with other prospective parents. They found out they were eligible, but that because Pat was in his early forties, they would have to adopt a slightly older child than they thought. The older parent was not to be more than forty years older than the child.

Pat and Jill came home and called a family meeting, asking the children what they wanted, a boy or a girl. Predictably, the boys wanted a boy and Karyn wanted a girl. Pat and Jill looked at each other. Why not? They applied for one of each. Another rule from the agency was that siblings would not be split up.

It was June before Pat and Jill learned that there was not a brother and sister pair available. But there was a pair of sisters. They talked it over with the kids who said to go for it. Then they had to wait. All they had seen were the orphanage pictures. The shooting down of the Korean airliner over the Soviet Union halted nearly all activity in Korea, and along with the usual adoption red tape, it would be fall before the Williamses would have any concrete news.

For months, Pat had to initiate everything in the marriage. Jill wasn't ready to send him cards, call him at the office, or implement B-E-S-T. "He had to be patient and persevere, and obviously it was God who gave him the strength to do it. And I'm glad he did."

Pat asked his old friend, Cleveland Indians scout and handcraft specialist Bobby Malkmus, to needlepoint B-E-S-T and a line from one of Jill's favorite songs, "You are the wind beneath my wings," for Jill. They hang in her kitchen and are constant reminders of Pat's commitment to continue to surprise her.

He also decided to run less and exercise more for upper-body strength. He now does four sets of pushups that total 160 a day, and, according to Jill, "He's a new man." He has also settled prayerfully the idea that he can read and study his Bible every day but that he needn't feel guilty if he doesn't get in a whole hour every time. He's come to believe the Old Testament admonition, "He that troubleth his own house shall inherit the wind . . ." (Proverbs 11:29 KJV), so his marriage and family have become top priority.

Pat insisted that Jill go with him to the 1983 NBA all-star game in Los Angeles. She was still a little gun-shy, but he helped arrange for a sitter because he had a few surprises cooked up for her on the West Coast. Two of her favorite radio preachers were Californians John MacArthur and Chuck Swindoll. Pat arranged for dinners with each of these men and their wives. Pat had flowers for Jill and treated her like a queen, so of course each couple was curious to know what was going on.

Both were fascinated and encouraged by the story. Chuck Swindoll encouraged Pat and Jill, "You've got to write a book. This story must be told. I've even got the title for it: *Rekindled.* Let me advise one more thing. Tell it all. Don't hold anything back. Tell it just as you've told it to us."

At the chapel service before the all-star game, Julius Erving of the Sixers introduced the speaker, former football great Roosevelt Grier. Rosie recounted how he had come to Christ after having broken up with his wife, and how his young son was instrumental in getting them back together. It couldn't have been more perfect for Pat and Jill that day.

Neither Pat nor Jill had a speaking or singing engagement in January, but their first obligation in February was a sweetheart banquet, of all things. Pat asked Jill to sing "Stubborn Love," a beautiful song that could be directed to God or to Pat. She asked what he was going to speak on.

"I think the time has come to talk about us," he said.

She caught her breath. She wasn't so sure. They weren't out of the woods yet. She certainly didn't feel comfortable about it. "Are you really going to do that?"

"Yes, I think we should."

"I was scared," Jill says. "I didn't know what it was going to do to me, especially sitting at the head table, facing the crowd."

First she sang "Stubborn Love": "Caught again, your faithless friend. Don't you ever tire of hearing what a fool I've been? Guess I should pray, but what can I say? Oh, it hurts to know the hundred times I've caused you pain. The 'forgive me's' sound so empty when I never change. Yet you stay and say 'I love you' still, forgiving me time and time again. It's your stubborn love that never lets go of me. I don't understand how you can stay, perfect love, embracing the worst in me. How I long for your stubborn love."*

Somehow, she got through it, but she couldn't look at Pat when he spoke. She wanted to look at the crowd and see how they were reacting, but soon she had to look down as the tears came. Pat was so honest, taking the blame, admitting he drove her to her difficult position and how he'd been a failure. But he also told what he'd learned from Dr. Ed Wheat's book, and many people asked where they could get it. To this day, Pat and Jill purchase *Love-Life for Every Married Couple* in large quantities and take them to every engagement.

Most impressive to Jill that night was Pat saying, "My wife has to be one of the most courageous people I've ever known, to finally be honest with me to the point where she got my attention. She didn't know how I'd react, what the outcome would be. Would I slap her? Kick her out? Ask for a divorce? She had no idea. She just knew I had finally asked what was wrong and seemed to really want to know, so she told me. And I thank God she did. The highest privilege in my life is being married to Jill."

"I was in tears, but so was the whole audience," Jill says. "They were wondering how Pat knew so much about their marriages. But he didn't. He just knew about ours, and apparently it had some universal problems. Over the next two years we would be overwhelmed with the stories we heard about Christian marriages breaking up, knowing how close we had come to the same result."

Jill felt a little sheepish about it, but part of her was glad that Pat had gone public with the story because she thought that might ensure his sticking with his new resolve. She was still worried, still scared.

For the weeks that followed, Pat called on every resource he had. He was pouring it on, living and dying for every ounce of encouragement he could eke out of Jill. "It had taken ten years to get to this," she says, "and it wasn't going to change overnight. Gradually I realized that I had to start giving too. I had to quit waiting for feelings and start willing myself to respond. When Pat acted out his love, he fell in love. That could happen to me too. And eventually it did."

In fact, it took Jill many months to get comfortable with the new Pat. With God's help, he had been patient. He held her hand in public, sat with his arm around her, looked at her, talked to her, listened to her, praised her, put her first. People started asking questions, and Pat was happy to tell them why he was publicly showing his love for his wife. "An outward show of affection wasn't a natural act for me," he admits. "But I did it. I had to do it. It didn't matter what people thought; it needed to be done."

At this time Pat memorized a key Scripture verse, Ephesians 5:25. Husbands are to love their wives, just as Christ also loved the church and gave himself for it. Christ loved the church so much he gave his life for it. What an example! The role of the husband is to be one of sacrificial devotion for his wife as he provides for her physical, emotional, psychological, and spiritual needs. A husband must love his wife enough to die for her.

Pat started rearranging his schedule so that he was studying his Bible at a convenient time for Jill and jogging on his lunch hour. At first he worried that he wouldn't have time to run as much, so he consulted with Dr. George Sheehan, a top running expert. "He said that a hundred and fifty to a hundred and eighty minutes a week is all your body needs. People who run more than that are running for their heads, not their bodies. So, I could cut down from eighty minutes a day to forty without hurting my training a bit." That way, when he was home, he was really home. And the independent macho image was gone. He was still a man, but man enough to help with the cooking, the dishes, the children—whatever needed to be done. Does he ever get tired of it? "It's hard work. But it's worth it." He and Jill go to bed together and wake up together fifteen minutes before the children so there's time to start the day with a good talk and lots of snuggling. The new motto around the house became, "I'd rather be snuggling."

The more Pat listened and learned about Jill, the more excited he became. He had not realized what a wonderful, deep, fascinating woman he was married to. When he let her be herself and brought out the best in her, the rewards were all his. He began to notice all her areas of creativity and spontaneity. "She's sharp and perceptive and valuable and interesting and intriguing. I mean, I never had any complaints, but now I know I've got more benefits than I ever dreamed I had."

Men often think in terms of investments. Put something into a project and by design and plan a dividend will return. Author and family expert Tim LaHaye says that a wife is the best investment a man can have. Everything he invests in her will be paid back in abundance and blessing.

Pat even got to the point where he decided that God had spoken to him many times through Jill. "With her sensitivity and her knowledge of our children and our home situation, she seems to have the inside track on many important decisions. When she suggests something, like having another baby, buying a van, moving, whatever, I start by assuming it's probably of God."

Significantly, other people noticed a difference in Pat's personality. He had more time to listen, to interact. He wasn't always running to another phone, or reading a sports page, or getting the subject back to his area of interest.

Pat even felt his new approach to marriage carried over in making him a better executive. His priority was his home, so he was forced to delegate more. He quit being a hands-in-everything manager and let his staff grow and develop. His people now have more authority and are more effective.

When Pat and Jill began working together on the B-E-S-T principles, they didn't just double the effectiveness, they multiplied it. They focused the same principles on Jimmy and Bobby and Karyn and saw almost immediate dramatic changes in their schoolwork, their relationships with each other, and their relationships with Pat and Jill. Karyn began demanding touching and hugging along with her good-night kiss, and soon all the kids did the same.

The first time Pat and Jill were apart after Pat's commitment to B-E-S-T was in March of 1983 when Jill took Jimmy to Israel for eleven days. Pat and Jill had been there before, and Jill wanted to go back, thinking it would be a wonderful experience for Jimmy, then eight. Their secretary, Barbara Albrecht, went too.

"It was a wonderful trip," Jill says, "and Jimmy and Barbara were fun to be with. I had a lot of old friends over there from the last time, and we did a lot of the same things as before. But I was a little out of sorts and I didn't know why. Something wasn't right. Something vague was bothering me.

"When I called Pat from Galilee one morning, I told him with some feeling that I really missed him. After that it got worse and I realized that I really didn't want to be away from him anymore. And it wasn't just all the great treatment I'd received. I missed *him*.

"By the second to last day of the trip, I was champing at the bit. The long flight to New York was almost unbearable. I thought it would never end. I hurried to the front of the line and rushed through customs. When I finally saw Pat I dissolved into tears. I missed him so much."

"That was the major turning point for me," Pat says. "I wasn't about to let up, but that emotional meeting evaporated my panic and let me settle in and love my wife without the fear of losing her after all."

Pat says, "We have a framework to handle whatever difficulties come along. I know that if Jill isn't happy, then I have failed to bless, edify, share, or touch, and I am driven right back to the fundamentals.

"I never want the memories of those dark days to leave me. Not that I ever want to go through them again. I'd rather die. But I want the memory to always be there. That's why we will always celebrate December 19 as an anniversary in our home. It marks the death of a marriage that had to die to allow the birth of one that had to be born."

Jill has become a much more understanding wife. Knowing that she is Pat's top priority, she understands and is eager to let him know it's all right when complications arise and he has to be late or has to be away from her at a ball game for a while. "It wasn't the incidents," she says. "It was the attitude. And I have no questions about that now. We just don't fight. I haven't felt the need to pout. If I have a problem, I tell him, and he listens. And we work on it. He won me back."

Epilogue

In June 1983, the Philadelphia 76ers paraded down Broad Street, with Pat and Jill and the children on one of the lead floats. Pat wouldn't have had it any other way. The world championship, without his wife and family, would have been empty.

In July, Pat shared the marriage story at Word of Life, where dozens of couples recommitted themselves to Christ and to each other. Later, a lovely Korean woman who had suffered under a demanding, authoritarian husband, told Pat in halting English that her husband broke down and cried, begging her forgiveness and promising to implement blessing, edifying, sharing, and touching in their marriage. "Do you think you can respond after all these years?" Pat asked.

"If he do that to me," she said tearfully, "how can I not respond?"

In September, a plane with precious cargo arrived from South Korea by way of Seattle and Minneapolis, and the baby girls, ages two and three, that Pat and Jill and the children had known and loved only by photo, were wearily delivered to them. Andrea and Sarah have added sweetness and joy to the Williams household above and beyond Pat and Jill's greatest expectations.

Any fear that the growth of the family might add too many pressures to a newly healed relationship is now fast receding.

Within days, they learned that Jill was pregnant. Nine months later, Pat, all five kids, and Jill's mom were in the delivery room to "assist" Dr. Brian Geary in Michael's delivery. The family was even. Three girls, and now three boys.

The Williams family is big, normal, happy, and radiant. Jill couldn't have dreamed of handling six children without a lot of help, and in spite of Pat's still terribly demanding schedule, they seem to be together most of the time.

On October 19, 1984, Pat and Jill prepared to leave for Word of Life again, looking forward to the first visit to the camp of Dr. and Mrs. Ed Wheat, who would be conducting a weekend marriage seminar. In the bathroom that morning, Pat found a two-day-early anniversary card addressed to "The *BEST* husband in the universe." Inside was an anniversary poem that Jill chose because it ended, "The best thing that ever happened to me is you," which she had underlined.

At the bottom, Jill had added in her own hand four of Pat's pet sayings, "Absolutely, Positively, Without a doubt, No question." And, "I love you, Jill."

Meeting Dr. Wheat face-to-face for the first time was a thrill. In the physician and marriage counselor Pat discovered a warm, Bible-loving man with a sweet, kind wife, Gaye. When Pat told him the whole story again and brought him up-to-date, the doctor told Pat to be ready "in case I call on you." The very next day Dr. Wheat called Pat to the platform to share his story.

The huge crowd was moved by Pat's honesty. But as he reached his dramatic conclusion, in which he had wanted to tell about the card he had received and contrast it with the devastating announcement Jill had made Christmas morning nearly two years before, his voice broke.

Pat had begun, "Twenty-two months ago this week," but before he could continue, emotion welled up inside. It was a first. He had never been overcome in front of a crowd in all his years of speaking, even since he had begun talking about the marriage. Pat waited for it to pass, then continued, "My wife sat up in bed and said, 'I'd rather be anywhere in the world than right here today.' "

He had to pause again, but this time the emotion would not subside. His voice thick, he hurried to conclude. "Yesterday Jill gave me a card and said she thinks I'm the greatest husband in the world." And then, weeping, "Thank you, Dr. Wheat." Overcome, he turned to the doctor, who stood and moved toward him, also in tears.

On December 19, 1984, two years to the day since the Darkest Hour, Pat and Jill Williams legalized their adoption of Andrea and Sarah in a courtroom in Mt. Holly, New Jersey, with all six children present. Later that night when Pat returned home from the Sixers game and tiptoed into the bathroom to prepare for bed, he found resting against his toothbrush a card with this message:

Dear Pat,
I love you so much for your response to that darkest hour two years ago today. And a large part of that response encompasses two Oriental dolls sleeping upstairs tonight. That you would share your name, life, and love with them is beyond their understanding . . . that you would share your name, life, love, and yourself *with me is truly my dream come true. There aren't enough words to express my love and devotion to you—I am the most blessed of all women.*
                                        Love,
                                          Jill

For Further Thought and Discussion

Chapter One: The Darkest Hour—a Confrontation

1. Did you ever experience a time of crisis in your marriage?
2. How did you handle it?
3. Have you ever suggested marital counseling and had your mate refuse? What reason was given?
4. How can one partner think a marriage is fine, while the other is thoroughly miserable?
5. What causes a person to refuse to acknowledge problems?
6. Can you be committed to marriage and yet fail to be committed to your spouse?
7. What steps can be taken when a spouse consistently refuses to acknowledge or deal with marital problems?

Chapter Two: Looking for Mr. Right

1. Did you feel pressured to marry by family, peers, society in general? If so, did this cause you to hurry into marriage? What effect has this had on your marriage?
2. Does a lack of self-esteem sometimes cause people to rush into marriage? Why?
3. Did physical attractiveness or public image influence your selection of a mate? Did this cause you to overlook other qualities? Did this cause problems later on?
4. Did you expect a mate to "make you happy"? Did you feel you

155

could not be happy in life unless and until you married? Did it occur to you that you were responsible for creating your own happiness?

5. Do you think you married for the wrong reasons? If so, what steps can you take to overcome any bad effect this has had on your married life?

6. Did you seek God's will in the selection of a life's partner? If yes, did you think that God would then take care of everything from that point on without effort on your part?

Chapter Three: Dating

1. Were your earlier relationships with the opposite sex awkward? If so, did you try to determine why?

2. Look back on your dating experiences. Do you see any pattern of behavior or reaction to your behavior that is being repeated in your marriage?

3. Could a fear of rejection resulting from a past romantic experience be keeping you from getting close to others, including your spouse?

4. If you did very little dating, do you think it has had an adverse effect on your marital adjustment?

5. Did you, during dating and courtship, fail to express yourself for fear of losing the other person? Did this become a pattern that held over into marriage? Or, conversely, was your spouse surprised by changes in your behavior?

Chapter Four: Self-Image

1. Do you lead a well-balanced life? Or are you so involved in one sphere that you neglect others? Could this be having an adverse effect on your marriage?

2. Is your self-image so wrapped up in your job, or perhaps in a hobby, that you neglect interpersonal relationships—especially in marriage?

3. Do you consider yourself a "loner"? Have you had close friends? Why not? How might this affect your marital adjustment?

4. Are you a person who needs to be in control? Do you tend to overplan and then overreact to unexpected events or disappointments? Are you flexible?

5. Are feelings of insecurity causing overdependence on your spouse for emotional support?

6. Do you check periodically to determine whether you are growing spiritually?

Chapter Five: Courtship

1. Did you marry without really getting to know your spouse? Why, because of an unusually short courtship or engagement?
2. Was your courtship and engagement period a happy one? How did you resolve any problems that came along? Are you still following the same pattern?
3. Did you accept your future spouse as he or she was?
4. Did you refuse to acknowledge negative thoughts about your loved one?
5. Did you expect to change qualities you disliked about your future mate? Did you?
6. Are there any special problems when a woman actively "pursues" a prospective mate? What are they?

Chapter Six: Preparing for Marriage

1. What expectations did you have for your marriage? Did you discuss them with your partner beforehand?
2. Have unmet expectations caused marital problems? Are the expectations reasonable?
3. Did you and your mate discuss before marriage such important matters as finances, careers, household duties, in-laws, children?
4. Did you and your spouse share in the wedding and honeymoon plans and the setting up of your first home? Or did one person by choice or by default take on the entire responsibility?
5. Was your honeymoon truly a time of being together? Was it sexually fulfilling? Was either partner restless? unable to relax? anxious to get back to "normal"?
6. Did you have premarital counseling? Was it helpful? Have you put to use what was learned through those meetings?

Chapter Seven: Adjustment

1. Once married, did you think the marriage would take care of itself without conscious effort? Why would you think that when other areas of life require continual effort?
2. Do you expect your spouse to make you happy? What problems might this cause?
3. What was the most difficult adjustment you had to make in marriage?
4. Have you always thought in terms of a partnership? of sharing

the good and the bad? Did you ever keep something important from your mate? Why? Did this cause more problems than it averted?

5. If one spouse has a difficult schedule, have you made a conscious effort to spend time together, giving each other full attention during that time?

6. What happened during your early married life that set the tone for the succeeding years? Think of both positive and negative things.

Chapter Eight: Priorities

1. Have you ever discussed priorities with your mate? Are you in agreement?

2. Is your spouse your top priority? Do you take her for granted? If your spouse is your top priority, do you make sure he knows it?

3. Does your mate complain that you do not pay attention, spend enough time together, or share common concerns and activities? Is the complaint valid? What have you done about it?

4. Do you enjoy yourself more in recreation or socially without your spouse? Why? What can both of you do to enjoy activities together?

5. Is your job your top priority? If your job takes most of your time and energy, is it because of the nature of the job or because of your own inability to gear down and do less? Is your job having an adverse effect on your marriage? What can you do about it?

6. Has your spouse been absent at a time of stress? For example, birth of a baby, illness or death of a family member? Did you make him aware of how important his presence and support would be?

Chapter Nine: Communication

1. Do you and your spouse communicate well? If not, what can be done to improve communication?

2. Do you think that if your mate cares for you, he will know how you feel and what you want without your saying so? Is this a reasonable attitude?

3. Do you want an emotional intimacy your spouse is not providing? Are you being understanding? Do you consider all the things that have gone into making him who he is? and why he acts as he does?

4. Does fear that opening up your innermost thoughts might bring about rejection prevent closeness in marital communication?

5. Have you ever refused to discuss something that was important to your partner—because it wasn't important to you?

6. How might simple differences in male/female attitudes be contributing to your communications problems?

7. Do you recognize that people have different ways of expressing love—and that it comes easy to some and is almost impossible for others? Do you realize that you may have to explicitly request certain expressions and in turn make an effort to give certain others?

Chapter Ten: Short-Term Solutions

1. Do the same disagreements come up over and over in your marriage?

2. What methods do you use to deal with disagreements? Are the solutions lasting or short-term?

3. Do you resort to the "silent treatment"? What does this accomplish? Why do you use this method?

4. Do you try to avoid conflict by refusing to be drawn into a marital disagreement? Do you realize that this can escalate the trouble?

5. Do you agree to almost anything in order to keep the peace and then go on as usual? Does this "postponement" solve any problems?

6. Do you draw back after initiating a confrontation, for fear of the consequences, thereby giving your mate mixed signals?

Chapter Eleven: Crisis

1. Do you realize that conflict is inevitable in marriage and that it is the response to it that determines success or failure?

2. Are you taking the long view, or are you letting the bad patches overwhelm you?

3. Do you think your marriage is over because you don't "love" your mate any longer? Was your marriage built on romantic feelings alone rather than romantic feelings plus commitment?

4. Are you blaming your marriage for distress in other areas of life, such as job, poor self-image, mid-life restlessness?

5. What steps should be taken by a couple whose marriage is in trouble?

6. Have you prayed about your marriage?

7. Have you sought outside help for marital problems. Why not?

Chapter Twelve: Commitment

1. Do you have a specific plan for rebuilding your marriage—not just good intentions? What is it?

2. If you and your spouse have agreed to work at your marriage, are you being patient about the progress? Are you sensitive to signs of effort on your mate's part?

3. When discouraged about your marriage, do you try to keep in mind the good things about your marriage and your spouse? What are they?

4. Do you insist that blame be assigned before working toward a better relationship? Is this destructive?

5. Have you thought about ways in which you might be contributing to marital problems? What are these ways?

6. Sometimes one partner must take the initiative in restoring a marriage. Are you able to do this? Can you move forward with a plan, with God's help alone, without promise of immediate return?

Chapter Thirteen: Toward Long-Term Healing

1. Have you sought biblical principles for guidance in marriage?

2. Do you bless your mate by speaking well of and to him? by doing kind things? by expressing appreciation verbally? by praying for her? How and how often?

3. Do you support and build up your spouse? How?

4. Do you share time, activity, interests, concerns, thoughts, goals, spiritual walk?

5. Do you express affection by nonsexual touching? How?

6. How often and for how long a period of time do you think these ideas have to be implemented to be effective?

7. Do you treat your spouse in a certain way because you believe it to be right, or to achieve certain ends?

Chapter Fourteen: Rekindled

1. What are the fundamentals of being a good marriage partner?

2. Do you accept the premise that you have to work at maintaining a good marriage?

3. What are you doing to nurture your marriage daily?

4. What framework have you worked out for handling problems as they come along?

5. Do you periodically recommit yourself to your marriage and to your spouse? In what specific ways do you do this?

Robert A. Cook:
Chancellor, The King's College
"Your heart will be warmed and your eyes wet with tears when you read how Pat and Jill Williams lost—and then found—each other, through consistent, loving, determined application of Scripture truth. Many a shaky marriage will be saved by a serious reading of Rekindled."

Ken Hatfield:
Head Football Coach, University of Arkansas
"I recommend it to engaged couples and newlyweds, so they may not make the tragic mistakes that many of us have and neglected those we love the most."

Ron Dick:
Philadelphia 76ers
". . . an intriguing story . . . advice for all, whether the relationship is in the early dating stages or if the couple has been married for fifty years."

David L. Hocking:
Senior Pastor, Calvary Church, Santa Ana, California
"The book Rekindled . . . is a powerful story because it exalts God's principles and gives hope to all who find themselves in marriages that are struggling and dying."

Harold Lindsell, Ph.D.:
Editor-emeritus, Christianity Today
"Rekindled . . . provides useful information on how the process of rebuilding can be started and how a new and fruitful marriage can be brought into being."

Bobby Bowden:
Head Football Coach, Florida State University
"Marriage is sacred, vital, and meant to be permanent. However, it's not easy and must be 'worked at.' This book is about two strong-willed people who 'worked it out.' . . . I recommend it to all couples."

John Wooden:
UCLA (Retired)
"I strongly recommend this story to every couple regardless of age or length of marriage."

Joseph C. Aldrich:
President, Multnomah School of the Bible
"A book of hope . . . . A classic, a valuable research tool which all will benefit from!"

Jack Wyrtzen:
Founder, Word of Life, Schroon Lake, New York
"I wish every married couple in America would read Rekindled—the divorce rate would drop dramatically."